Mother Nurture

Stephanie Hirsch

WITH HANNAH SELIGSON

Mother Nurture

Life Lessons from the Mothers of America's Best and Brightest

wm WILLIAM MORROW *An Imprint of* HarperCollins*Publishers*

Grateful acknowledgment is made to the following for the use of the photographs appearing in this book:

Alicia Keys (current), page 137, by Kevin Mazur. Justin Timberlake (current), page 297, by Kevin Mazur. Christopher Bridges aka Ludacris (current), page 49, by Donna Parnell. John Legend (childhood), page 162, by Eric Gregory, reprinted courtesy of the *Springfield News-Sun*. Diane Sawyer (current), page 245, by Ida Mae Astute. Uma Thurman (current), page 291, by Dimitrios Kambouris. Nikki Taylor (childhood), page 284, by Sean Renaro; Nikki Taylor (current), page 285, by Ken Taylor. Mary Higgins Clark (current), page 127, by Blair M. Relyea. Beyoncé Knowles (current), page 151, by Cliff Watts.

HarperCollins books may be purchased for educational, business, or sales promotional use. For information please write: Special Markets Department, HarperCollins Publishers, 10 East 53rd Street, New York, NY 10022.

FIRST EDITION

Designed by Janet Evans and Nicola Ferguson

Library of Congress Cataloging-in-Publication Data has been applied for.

ISBN 978-0-06-118920-3

08 09 10 11 12 WBC/RRD 10 9 8 7 6 5 4 3 2 1

To Hunter: My beautiful boy who has made my heart so much bigger. My love for you is endless. Momma is always here for you.

To Izzy: My loyal friend and husband who's selfless love has given me the wings to fly. You have made my dreams reality. Thank you.

CONTENTS

Mother Nurture

INTRODUCTION

I vividly remember that afternoon in a way that only someone whose life has been dramatically altered by the birth of a child can. It is ingrained in my memory since it was the first time in the days following the birth of my son, Hunter, that I had any sense of self. And although I should have been savoring a much-needed moment of solitude, I was overcome with doubt and questions that I had pushed aside in lieu of feeding Hunter and changing his diaper.

At that instant, all I could think about was, how did Steven Spielberg's mother do it? How did she raise such a well-rounded son who has risen to the zenith of his chosen profession, manifests his generosity through countless philanthropic pursuits, and is a happily married dad on top of it all? How did Mrs. Adler raise such a mensch—a man with admirable characteristics like fortitude, a big heart, and the courage of his convictions?

I had to know.

But Leah Adler was just the tip of the iceberg. I wanted to know—in fact, I had to know: what did the mothers of these successful people—the movers and shakers who have gone on to define their generation, to break world records, and to leave irreparable marks in their respective fields—do to help their children get where they are today? I started to think about all of the mothers I wanted to question. How did Terri Augello, Alicia Keys's mother, raise a nine-time Grammy Award–winning daughter, who is also active in many charitable organizations that inspire and encourage American youth? What did Linda Armstrong Kelly, Lance Armstrong's mother, do to raise a seven-time Tour de France winner who battled testicular cancer and then went on to win the Tour two more times after that? How did Gladys Clash, Kevin Clash's mother, help him cultivate the artistic talent that led him to create the iconic Elmo character? What did Jean Hayes, Diane Sawyer's mother, do to contribute to her rise from a local reporter in Kentucky to anchor of ABC's *Good Morning America*? And how did Dot Jeter, Derek Jeter's mother, raise a son who has the sixth-highest lifetime batting average as well as his own charity to encourage young people to stay away from drugs and alcohol?

I craved the answers to these questions because, like any new parent, my time was consumed by my work and my family. But my brain was constantly rattling with questions about parenting. Will that sugary cereal really influence his eating habits for the rest of his life? Does an extra hour of television on weekends mean he'll struggle as a reader when he reaches third grade? What can I do—realistically—to give him the best childhood possible? How can I, as a mother, build the best foundation for the adult he will become?

I didn't have time to sift through countless parenting books. Moreover, I wasn't interested in hypotheses about how to parent. I wanted concrete examples of how real mothers of successful people had raised their children. And so, I began writing *Mother Nurture*. No matter what race, religion, or socioeconomic status, *we are all mothers* and we all have the same goal as parents: we want our children to be successful in life; "success" can mean different things to everyone. Children's success might mean to get the best education they can, to be inspired and fulfilled by their careers, to get married and have children, or to give back to the community. Whatever your definition of success is, as parents we all want the best for our children.

Of course, nurture is only part of the equation, and *Mother Nurture* is certainly not a scientific, psychological, or sociological study of motherhood. I think I even missed Psychology 101! Rather, it is my gift to regift what I learned through conversations with fifty-two mothers of the most driven, creative, and philanthropic people in this country.

Writing this book illustrated to me what any parent in the twenty-first century knows. Parenthood—not to mention childhood—has fundamentally changed. And while many modern advances—from disposable diapers to microwavable chicken nuggets to an abundance of educational and entertaining DVDs—make motherhood today easier, it has also gotten a lot more complicated. During so many of my conversations with these mothers, we would talk about a time when there wasn't such a thing as "organized play," educational television was limited to *Sesame Street*, and enrichment classes were pretty much just ballet lessons or after-school sports.

Contrast that with today. I worry that if I give Hunter a cookie, he'll get addicted to sugar and grow up to be obese. I'm scared that if I am not constantly trying to stimulate him, or that if he watches TV, he'll grow up to be lazy and unmotivated. My husband and I are so busy working to provide him with all the things he needs, I'm sometimes concerned that we're not giving him the one thing he needs most—us.

This is not a "how to" book. Taken as a blueprint, a road map, or system to make your child the next big baseball player (or lawyer, or doctor, or CEO), the point is lost. Instead, my hope is that you'll take from this book a collage of perspectives. Maybe you'll draw inspiration from Uma Thurman's mother's Buddhist approach to parenting, or from how Mary Aigner, the mother of Julie Aigner-Clark, the founder of the Baby Einstein empire, took her daughter to the library every Friday, or from the innovative way Madeline McElveen, the mother of Red Cross president Bonnie McElveen, taught her how to cross the street.

Whatever it is, I know this is a gift that will keep giving.

Mary Aigner

Mother of JULIE AIGNER-CLARK

"Just do well and be your own person."

*M*ary Aigner—the mother of Julie Aigner-Clark, whose brainchild Baby Einstein has become a household name and revolutionized the baby toy industry—said that Julie was born under a lucky star. "Things pretty much always went well for Julie," Mary said. Julie, the founder of the Baby Einstein Company, sold the organization to the Walt Disney Company in 2001. Her company was the first to produce developmental media, including DVDs, music CDs, books, and toys that focus on the arts and humanities, for very young children. Julie is also founder of the children's media company the Safe Side, which is responsible for the three-time Emmy Award—winning videos *Stranger Safety* and *Internet Safety*. Julie and her companies have been featured on *The Oprah Winfrey Show*, *Live with Regis and Kelly*, and *Entertainment*

Tonight as well as in the *New York Times*, the *Wall Street Journal*, and *Parenting* magazine. Julie has received numerous awards for her work, including Ernst & Young's Entrepreneur of the Year Award; *Working Mother*'s Entrepreneur of the Year Award, in three categories; and the Distinguished Alumni Award from Michigan State University for starting a billion-dollar industry focused on stimulating the minds of infants and toddlers. In 2007, Julie was personally honored by President Bush at the State of the Union address. Julie donates to a number of organizations but has been particularly active with the National Center for Missing and Exploited Children (www.missingkids.com). In addition, Julie is involved with the Elephant Sanctuary in Hohenwald, Tennessee; the World Wildlife Fund; the Gathering Place (a local shelter for women and children in Denver); and the Logan School for Creative Learning. Julie continues to teach middle-school literature and lives in Colorado with her husband and two daughters.

Julie was a planned pregnancy for Mary, as was her choice to only have one child. Explaining her decision, Mary said, "We just didn't want a lot of kids. We just felt we wanted to have one child, so we could do everything for this one child." Mary worked through part of her pregnancy, but then stayed home with Julie during her formative years. "I stayed home with Julie by choice and raised her for seven years. . . . I wanted to be there with Julie during those first years." Later, as a working mom, Mary said that sometimes she felt guilty about splitting her time between Julie and the office, but made a point to be there for the big moments. "The first day of school was a big deal in our neighborhood. All the mothers walked their kids to school. . . . I always went to work late that day because I walked Julie to school with the other mothers."

Mary said Julie was "always a reader," as might be expected from someone who has built an empire centered on education. "We would go to the library every Friday, probably from the time she was two years old, and Julie would pick out the books she wanted to bring home for the week. . . . It was our Friday routine. We went to the library and then went to lunch." Mary stressed, however, that she didn't push Julie. "I took the approach that if she was ready, it would come naturally to her." Like her daughter, Mary was also innovative about the tools she used to teach. "I thought that TV with direction could be an excellent learning tool. In fact, I personally learn something every day from television." Mary, however, did not just expose Julie to the things that she enjoyed. Even though Mary said she "wasn't big on classical music," she played it for Julie growing up. "I thought it was important for her to have a broad appreciation of music." But Julie wasn't always stimulated, Mary said. "Julie was an only child, so she learned how to play by herself, which I thought was important. She didn't need to have commotion all the time."

Mary placed an enormous value on education and learning. However, that didn't mean sending Julie to expensive schools. "We decided to raise her in Grosse Point, Michigan, because they had one of the best public school systems around. . . . I wanted her to have exposure to different kinds of people. We could have afforded to send her to private school, but we chose not to."

When it came to expectations, Mary said that she didn't pressure Julie to succeed. "Of course I wanted her to do very well, but I never said, 'Julie, I want you to be this or that.'" Still, Mary believed that children need a certain amount of discipline and direction. "I always saw my role as a guide. One area where I prodded a little more was when it came to education. I made it very clear to Julie that she should go to college. I wanted to make sure that she could earn a living and not be dependent on us or a man," advice that Julie has certainly internalized.

Encouragement, Mary said, was a staple of her parenting style. "I constantly said to Julie, 'We are so proud of you. That's so great.'" Crediting her forty-three-year marriage as the core of her family, Mary said, "It was my marriage that made us such a strong family unit. We had so much love for each other," a love that was manifested in both the big things and the little things. "We always ate dinner together," Mary said. "Even though I worked, I'd come home and we would have dinner as a family. More importantly, we would talk about the day. . . . I talked about my job and all the people I worked with. . . . I made them laugh with my stories." Religion in the Aigner household was not practiced through rituals, but rather through actions: "I think we just showed religion through love and appreciation of each other on a daily basis."

For Mary, goals were not some lofty ideals. They were things she thought about concretely and frequently. "I had personal goals for Julie. I wanted to make sure that she was happy and that she had a lot of friends, and that she had exposure to different things." Part of engaging Julie with different things included bringing her along to what were typically "adult only" activities. "I was not the type of parent who said, 'Let's get a babysitter'; Julie always came on vacation with us. . . . I didn't want to leave her." As a result, Julie visited a wide variety of places. "We traveled to Europe every other year, and, locally, we used to go to the art museum in Detroit." Putting herself in the neutral zone in terms of discipline—somewhere between strict and laid-back—Mary said that manners were her main cause. "I wanted Julie to have good manners and say 'please' and 'thank you.'"

Reminiscing, Mary said that she first saw something special in Julie when she was seven years old. "She would just sit at the kitchen table and write poems, and the school always entered her in competitions. We had the *Detroit Free Press* at the time, and a few times a year kids could submit short stories or poetry and they always entered Julie's stuff. She usually won a prize." Mary said that she and her husband would help Julie with her writing, but emphasized, "It was really her own thing. . . . I would help her with her writing. . . . Her dad would suggest changing a sentence around here or there. . . . But we didn't push her."

Mary's main priorities as a parent were about making sure that

Julie felt grounded and secure. "I just wanted her to have a good solid feeling about life and just be happy to be herself. I told her, 'Just do well and be your own person.'" Mary said it's a point that she can't stress enough. "I always made it clear that even if she had some hard knocks, it's okay because we'll help you with it. Julie doesn't need us financially or anything like that anymore, but to this day she knows that she can always, always count on us."

Linda Armstrong Kelly

Mother of LANCE ARMSTRONG

"If you shelter your children, you don't really do them any favors."

*L*inda Armstrong Kelly—the mother of Lance Armstrong, seven-time winner of the Tour de France—said that in interviews, when the topic turns to his mother, Lance will say, "She's a tough lady"—a quality you might expect from a mother who raised a son as accomplished as Lance Armstrong. At seventeen, Lance was invited to train with the Junior National Cycling Team. Lance then went on to be a top amateur cyclist after the 1992 Barcelona Olympics. By the mid-1990s, Armstrong had won the Tour DuPont twice and was hailed as the United States's finest cyclist. But Lance's life has hardly been all medals and good fortune—in 1996, Lance discovered that he had testicular cancer, which spread extensively. After chemotherapy and surgery, Lance returned to cycling in 1997 and eventually went on to win his first Tour de France two years later.

Lance's athletic success, dramatic recovery from cancer, and philanthropic activities inspired the Lance Armstrong Foundation, a charity founded in 1997. Together with Nike he launched the high-end cycling clothing collection 10/2 (which refers to the day he was diagnosed with cancer). Part of the proceeds are donated to the Lance Armstrong Foundation. Additionally, in 2004, the foundation developed the Livestrong wristband in conjunction with Nike, to support cancer victims and survivors and to raise awareness about cancer. As of the beginning of 2006, over fifty-eight million wristbands had been sold. Lance has been named Sportsman of the Year by *Sports Illustrated*, Associated Press Male Athlete of the Year four years in a row, and BBC Sports Personality of the Year Overseas Personality; he also has received ESPN's ESPY Award for Best Male Athlete. Lance is the father of three children: Luke, Isabelle, and Grace.

Lance's life has been defined, in large part, by beating the odds and surviving in difficult circumstances—approaches modeled for him by his mother. Linda was an extremely young mother—she had Lance at seventeen—who was raised in a low-income family with an alcoholic father. Reflecting on her early years, Linda said, "We learned how to work at a very young age, even before it was legal to work. A couple of things came from that. I learned how to be a survivor as well as how to have that fire in the belly, and that gave me the real desire to be able to get ahead." However, Linda did more than just *think* about these things—she actualized these principles. "When I had Lance, we had no insurance, so I had a paper route that I threw in the middle of the night. I'd go to school during the day, and that's what paid the rent. I didn't take any public assistance." Linda also said she modeled a "roll with the punches" attitude, as raising a son as a single, teenage mother was a far cry from the Donna Reed life she had imagined. At the end of the day, Linda said, she made the best of it.

Looking at Linda, the connection between Lance's positive attitude and resiliency is a clear line. Describing how she went to work even with no skills and got her GED, she said, "I was just grateful for any work that I could have. It was usually working in offices, and I made minimum wage." When times got tougher, Linda took the initiative to remove herself from a situation that she described as "abusive." Always imagining a better life for Lance and herself, Linda said, "I did not want my son to grow up in an abusive home." Using the phrase that she's repeated thousands of times over the years, Linda said that her attitude about that situation was (and is): "No matter what it took, I was going to make it."

Although Linda was quite young when she had Lance, she described a parenting philosophy well beyond her years. "I understood that you are in charge of the destiny of both you and your child. . . . It wasn't just about giving him material things. It was about what I could show him." Linda emphasized, too, the great satisfaction she found in parenting, saying, "There was so much joy and happiness in the purpose and meaning of being a mother."

Like many single mothers, Linda had to support Lance on scarce resources. "We had a one-bedroom apartment, and I supported Lance on $400 a month." As might be expected from the most famous cyclist in the world, Lance hit all the developmental benchmarks way ahead of schedule. "He walked at nine months, he was potty trained at eighteen months, and he tied his shoes at two." Even though Linda was working hard, she still dedicated her life to Lance. "I would work, but the evenings and weekends were devoted to Lance. We did a lot of things outside. Lance and I would go to the swimming pool in the apartments. . . . He loved outdoor stuff." Taking steps to cultivate his innate athletic talent, Linda signed Lance up for football and soccer from the time he was six.

Instead of pushing Lance to pursue a certain sport, Linda's approach was more to let him figure out what he was good at. "I think you have to help kids find their passion. . . . Once they find it, you've got to really focus on it. In Lance's case, he realized that he wasn't a great football player or baseball player, but that he was good at running and swimming, which I realized when he started doing triathlons at fourteen." To help him develop as a runner and swimmer, Linda would get up every weekend to take Lance to his races. More than focusing on winning these races, Linda said she made it about setting a goal. "I just felt like it wasn't important to stress winning all the time because you don't win all the time." Her expectations really boiled down to ethics, morals, values, and how you treat people.

Linda's parenting style was defined largely by helping Lance cultivate his independence. "I wasn't packing his bags for him when he went to triathlons," she said. "I wasn't reminding him to get his goggles, his swimsuit, and his equipment and all that because I figured, you know, if he doesn't show up, that's his problem. So I didn't baby him in that respect. He realized that he had to be responsible. My role was to drive us there, get a hotel, get the food, and to cheer him on." It was this sense of ownership over his own life that Linda said was paramount to helping Lance get where he is today. "If we had to go to a different race, I would say, 'Okay Lance, you need to find directions on how to get there.' I mean, he was literally driving to Tulsa, Oklahoma, when he was fifteen with me in the car and getting us back home. . . . I just thought if you shelter your children, you don't really do them any favors." Linda makes no mistake, however, about the priority she put on Lance: "My son was my number one commitment."

Although Lance didn't have a strong male role model growing up, Linda made sure to create a close family atmosphere between the two of them. "I was mom. I was father. I was friend. I was the rock. . . . Every night I felt like it was important to sit down and have dinner together. So we would sit down every night and talk about the day and what we were going to do that weekend. Even at ten years old he was telling me about different races that he wanted to train for."

In line with her involved parenting style, Linda said Lance's childhood was very orderly. "I would say Lance had quite a bit of structure growing up; he was always in bed by nine." Understanding the cardinal tenet of parenting a teenager, Linda said that she definitely learned to pick her battles with Lance. However, this hardly meant that she tolerated bad behavior. "I wasn't a nagger . . . but I always told him you have choices in life and you know these are choices that will have consequences. . . . We'd talk a lot. We had a lot of communication."

A vivid example of how Linda helped Lance tap into his enormous arsenal of talents is the way Linda encouraged her son to actually write down his goals. "It taught him so much. . . . Then I got him a Rolodex and had him start collecting business cards from people. He was only fourteen years old." Linda also credits outlook as a key part of helping Lance get where he is today. Despite the hardships that life dealt her, Linda said she always maintained a positive attitude—a quality Lance certainly internalized. "I just always, always encouraged the optimistic part of life." Reflecting on how this impacted Lance, Linda said, "When Lance had cancer, he didn't look at himself as a statistic. He didn't have to look at the fact that people die from this because he knew he was different. He was not going to give in to this disease."

Above all, Linda said her parenting style was, and is, defined by not trying to keep up with the Joneses. "We never felt like, 'Hey, I want to be like that person,' because that's not the reality." Linda just encouraged Lance to focus more on his *own* success. "I always told Lance to set your expectations and goals really high because that gives you something to reach for. . . . I told him make this the first day of the rest of your life." Today, Linda doesn't take credit for all Lance has accomplished; she said that she just helped him, at a young age, find his passion, stay focused, and really pushed him to the next level. As for Linda's advice to mothers who want to guide their children to successful lives: "It's so easy. It's three things: love, support, and nurture."

Eva Balazs

Mother of ANDRÉ BALAZS

"The idea of planning things and being anxious just didn't exist."

*E*va Balazs—the mother of hotel mogul André Balazs—said that when André was a child, she always wondered what he was going to do with his life because he was so good at so many things. "It was always clear to me, though, that he wasn't going to be a scientist." She was certainly right about that. André Balazs has created some of the most innovative and widely imitated hotels in the world, including the luxury Mercer hotel in New York; Hollywood's famed Chateau Marmont; the Standards Hotels in Hollywood and downtown L.A.; the Standard Spa in Miami Beach; and the seaside hideaway Sunset Beach on Shelter Island. He recently renovated the 1940s oceanfront classic the Raleigh in Miami, its fleur-de-lis pool heralded as "one of the sexiest hotel pools in America" by *Condé Nast Traveler,* and opened the ultramodern and affordable Hotel QT, located in the heart of Times Square, New York.

André has expanded his empire to include residential developments for which he has collaborated with some of the world's most renowned architects, such as Jean Nouvel, Richard Gluckman, and Calvin Tsao. André Balazs Hotels have earned an impeccable national and international reputation, having been featured in all major publications, including *Vanity Fair, Travel & Leisure,* the *New York Times, Architectural Digest,* and *Vogue.* André is the father of two daughters and resides in Manhattan, New York.

Eva described herself by saying, "I was a full-time mother. . . . I went to college in Budapest, Hungary, and studied liberal arts, but didn't work when I had my two children—André and his sister, Maryanne." Eva recalled that "reading was the most pleasant time of my day. . . . I would read all the classical childhood books to André—everything from *Babar* to *Charlotte's Web.*" In fact, Eva said that reading was the nightly ritual that took the place of TV. She credited her strict "no TV policy" for fostering a more communicative and intellectual environment in her house. "I think because we didn't have TV there was more reading and talking. The three of us always ate dinner together." It was during these nightly family dinners that Eva said, "We'd discuss what happened at school, and what everyone was reading about." Most things, as Eva described them, happened organically in the Balazs household. Asked about whether she was anxious about André hitting certain milestones, she said, "No, the idea of planning things and being anxious just didn't exist."

Although there was a strict no TV policy, the Balazs household was hardly devoid of entertainment. "I played the piano a lot, and music was an important part of André's upbringing," Eva recalled. When it came to activities and scheduling things, she again emphasized how they happened without much thought. "I remember I used to ride my bike around a lake and I would give André crayons and he would just sit and draw while I did whatever it was I was do-ing." Along those lines, Eva stressed that she would never push activities, only suggest things. Some things, however, such as ath-letics, were scheduled. "We were very much into sports," Eva ex-plained. "My husband and I played tennis on the local, public tennis courts; we also did square dancing. . . . Sports were a different world then," Eva remembered. "You didn't have to sign your child up. They just happened right there in the neighborhood. Things were much more laid-back."

As Eva described it, family and friends were interchangeable. "My friends were such a huge part of my life that they were really like family. I never took them for granted."

Eva's parenting style was about using the everyday things, like taking care of a dog, to impart the bigger life lessons. "When André got a dog, I told him, 'You are responsible for the welfare of this lit-tle creature. You need to be kind and good to it, and the same goes for nature. You don't cut down a tree just because it's there. It's a liv-ing thing. Be respectful, kind, and protective toward those who need you." Praise and encouragement were also staples of Eva's parenting approach. "I wasn't the type of mother who said, 'I love you' all the time. But I definitely gave him a lot of hugs and kisses." Even today, at the top of his field, Eva said she still gives him a lot of praise and encouragement.

Since André was a child who had so many talents, Eva felt it was difficult to single out his special traits, but said his confidence was something that always stood out. "He was very self-assured, but sometimes that was hard for me as a parent. He could not be cajoled or threatened." Eva said she dealt with André's strong will by just always emphasizing responsibility. "There is really not that much you can do, except just tell a child that it's their responsibility." And while it was difficult at times to raise a child with such determina-tion, Eva credits André's self-assurance for helping him get where he is today. "I remember seeing this quality in him from the time he was very young. I remember he was playing by himself in a sand-box when he was about four years old and two older boys, who were about seven and eight, came by and started talking down to him, and André looked up into the eyes of one of the boys who was standing very close to him and then André said something and the two boys walked away." Realizing the enormous upside of his self-assurance and determination, Eva said she had to walk a fine line between not squelching this trait and, at the same time, setting limits.

When André was sixteen, his parents got divorced. Eva said it was a "tough time, and a particularly hard time for André, who was smack in the middle of his adolescence." Asked how she helped her son weather seeing his parents' marriage dissolve, Eva said, "I've, first and foremost, realized that time is a great healer. I also think our close relationship helped get us through it. We love each other very much. Most importantly, he just knew that I was there for him, and that I always will be."

Nancy Golden

Mother of NATE BERKUS

"You can't box your children in. If they don't follow the road you
had planned for them in your head, get yourself a new map
and buckle up for an unpredictable, sometimes terrifying,
and hopefully wonderful journey."

J was the only kid on the block who knew about furniture scale by
the time I was eight," says Nate Berkus, founder of the world-
renowned interior design firm Nate Berkus Associates, which
he founded at the age of twenty-four. Clearly that wherewithal has
served him well, something he can thank his mother, Nancy Golden,
for. Nancy, an interior designer, is now the host of a design show on
the DIY Network. Although Nancy says she never assumed Nate would
enter the field, the decision to follow in her footsteps didn't surprise
her. "He saw how happy I was being an interior designer and how helping people live well had a positive impact on both me and my clients."

Today, Nate's impact is being felt far and wide. His firm has worked on projects as diverse as Wolfgang Puck's restaurant Spago, Barney's New York, and W Hotels. In 2001, Nate was invited to make over a small space for *The Oprah Winfrey Show*. That opened the door for him to become a featured design expert for the show, and he continues as a regular contributor to *O at Home* magazine. Nate has also recently taken his aesthetic to the masses. Linens 'n Things has launched a complete line of Nate Berkus products for the home. Nate's first book, *Home Rules: Transform the Place You Live into a Place You'll Love* (Hyperion), was released in 2005. To fully round out his multimedia empire, Nate debuted with an XM radio on the *Oprah & Friends*'s channel.

Nate, the oldest of Nancy's three children, was not planned, she says. "I was twenty-three years old when he was born. I was a baby having a baby." Early in Nate's life, Nancy says her life was thrown into upheaval. "I got divorced and remarried again in the same year." Asked how the divorce impacted her relationship with Nate, Nancy says she gave him a lot of attention as a result. "I felt guilty over the divorce."

Even with three young kids, Nancy always worked. "I wanted my own income and identity." For Nancy, interior design was not just a job, it was a passion. "I loved it, and I went back to night school for interior design while I was pregnant. Then I started working for myself three days a week." Nancy says she was able to forge her career with the force she did because of the wonderful help she had. "I found a stay-at-home grandmother of seven who was looking to get out of her apartment. She worked for our family for twenty years. She and her husband became surrogate grandparents."

Reflecting on Nate's early development, Nancy says his verbal skills "were frightening." However, she didn't track his milestones. "I knew he was bright and very precocious. I heard it every day from strangers." Although you might think that someone with Nate's acumen had a strict educational regimen growing up, Nancy says they didn't even have a reading ritual. "When we did read, which happened informally, they were standard children's books. Today, Nate is a voracious reader, go figure." Describing a laid-back atmosphere to Nate's upbringing, Nancy says she never enforced strict rules about TV. But that hardly meant that they were couch potatoes. "We spent a lot of time biking and going to the neighborhood lake," Nancy recalls. "He also attempted to play Little League baseball, but spent most of the time in right field waving to me."

Although Nate went to Hebrew school three days a week, Nancy says his upbringing was more culturally than religiously Jewish. Still unsure about whether Nate actually made it to Hebrew school (Nancy just saw that he got on the bus), she says what she remembers most about Nate's relationship with Judaism was the amount of time they spent picking out his outfit for his bar mitzvah.

Even at the behest of many people that Nate audition to be a model, Nancy says she never had any intention of becoming a stage mom. "I took him to one modeling audition when he was about thirteen. After that, if he wanted to try it, he had to wait until he could drive and get himself to auditions." As for how she was able to take a step back from Nate's life, she credits it to the big expectations he had for himself. "He didn't need a pushy mother."

Describing her general parenting style as a smorgasbord, Nancy says she went from lenient, nurturing, and sympathetic to invasive and short. It's why she maintains that Dr. Spock, the parenting guru, "would have flunked me." What was always consistent, however, was the belief and pride she had in her son. "I am his greatest cheerleader." Like most Jewish mothers, Nancy says the affection and accolades come in steady streams. "I never stop with the kisses and hugs." With a bond as close as Nancy and Nate's, she says it's still just as sad saying good-bye to him today as it was sending him on a plane for the first time, taking him to boarding school, or dropping him off at college. "As an adult, I still tear up when we split. Our times to reconnect just seem so far apart!"

Nancy maintains that it's a quartet of things—talent, a hard work ethic, a big heart, and a little luck—that has gotten Nate where he is today. While he always showed an interest in interior design—Nancy says he'd been redoing his room since he was young—she thought he'd end up in fashion. But with Nate's enormous arsenal of talents, Nancy says the world was his oyster. "He was fearless in his belief in himself. He honed his people skills and was excited by the unknown. He also has tremendous coping skills and a ton of common sense."

Everywhere he went, not only did he succeed, but he shined. "School grades were always important to him, but he did well because he wanted to. If he screwed up, it's because he chose to." Asked how she dealt with his slipups, Nancy says she does believe in punishment. "I would ground him and have him babysit his brother and sister, which was reason enough to behave." Although Nate always got good grades in high school, it was a somewhat trying time for him, Nancy remembers. "Nate decided to apply to boarding school because he wasn't happy with the local school. He applied and was accepted to all three, and was the single student asked to speak at graduation. Needless to say, I sobbed through that one."

Pinpointing the defining moments in Nate's life, Nancy says there are a library of them, but one does stick out. "I guess the loudest one was sitting in my family room with eleven girlfriends watching Nate on *Oprah* for the first time. I was cheering, laughing, and crying. We all knew we were watching a star being born right in front of us. It was surreal." Asked about how she helped Nate get where he is today, Nancy says it's due, in part, to letting go of expectations. "You can't box your children in. If they don't follow the road you had planned for them in your head, get yourself a new map and buckle up for an unpredictable, sometimes terrifying, and hopefully wonderful journey."

Drawing a picture of herself, Nancy says that Nate grew up watching a mother who loved her family, friends, and career, but also one who has had to continually prove her resiliency. "I had to deal with adversity and disappointment, but I always kept a sense of humor and would make fun of myself." It was all of these qualities—and more—that Nancy says she had to harness when tragedy struck Nate's life in 2004 after his boyfriend, Fernando, was killed in Thailand during the tsunami. "I have never felt more useless as a mother," Nancy recalls about that devastating period. "Watching your child suffer and not being able to put a Band-Aid on the wound is true heartache." But it was some formative advice during that period of intense loss that Nancy says made an indelible impression on how she sees her role as a mother today. "A therapist told me that when you breathe, you breathe oxygen, but you don't think about it, you just do it. 'You're Nate's oxygen,' he told me. 'You don't need to do anything more than be there. It's not anything you say. It's just your presence that supports and helps him.' " Today, Nancy says Nate has been able to recover. "He is in a wonderful and loving relationship, and I can see that his wounds are healing."

Gladys Bettis

Mother of JEROME "THE BUS" BETTIS

"It was always my philosophy that he was blessed and therefore he was obligated to give back."

Gladys Bettis—the mother of Jerome Bettis, who is considered to be one of the greatest running backs in NFL history—said having been raised with eight brothers (yes, eight!) and seeing them use her dolls as footballs, she swore if she had a son he wasn't going to play football. Looking back today, Gladys said, "So it was both ironic and unbelievable what's happened with Jerome." *Unbelievable* certainly rings true. In 1993, Jerome was selected in the first round of the NFL draft for the Los Angeles Rams. That same year he won rookie of the year, Rams MVP, the *Sporting News* Rookie of the Year, and won the Super Bowl with the Steelers and now appears on *Football Night in America* as a top sports commentator.

In addition to his illustrious football career, Jerome established Jerome Bettis Enterprises in 1997 as a full-service sports marketing firm. The company has been involved with many national marketing campaigns, including Nike, Ford, and EA Sports. Using his own experience with asthma as the platform, Jerome teamed up with pharmaceutical company GlaxoSmithKline to start an asthma awareness campaign. But Jerome's advocacy work hardly stops there. Jerome also founded The Bus Stops Here Foundation, a not-for-profit organization. He has established a scholarship program for seniors graduating from his former high school, McKenzie High, and he returns to his former camp every year to host the legendary Reggie McKenzie Football Camp. Jerome and his wife, Trameka, have two children—Jada and Jerome Jr.

Since Jerome was the youngest of three children, Gladys said she didn't worry much about his developmental milestones. "I had two other kids, so I knew what to expect. He started to walk at about eleven or twelve months and talk around a year and a half, which were totally normal for a boy." As part of her easygoing approach, Gladys said she wasn't the type of mother to sit down and initiate playtime. "I would just let them play. I didn't think playtime had to be structured," she said.

The structured activity in the Bettis household was bowling. "We had weekly family bowling outings. All the kids learned to bowl and were actually exceptionally good at it." Gladys said that what started as a sport she encouraged her children to play because it was safe became an activity rife with life lessons. "I've been reading through some of Jerome's biographies and he wrote about how much he learned from bowling—the experience of working with a team, not to mention all of the math he had to learn just to keep score."

When reflecting on the expectations she had for Jerome growing up, Gladys said she was always confident in his abilities and didn't think too long or hard about what he would become. "He was just extremely smart—a member of the National Honor Society—so I never really questioned his abilities." And although she didn't have concrete expectations for Jerome in terms of accomplishing specific goals, she described herself as a "stickler" about education. "In the Bettis house, you had to go to school, be there on time, and show up every day. Even if you didn't feel well, you still had to go to school. I definitely pushed him to get good grades." Gladys said Jerome's education also included lessons in how to be a gentleman. "I taught Jerome and his brother to open doors for women."

Even though Gladys described herself as the stronger parental figure, Jerome's father—Gladys's husband of forty-one years—was a significant role model in his life. "Jerome's father was a very important role model for him, because he was always at home. He set an excellent example. He didn't smoke, he didn't drink, and he didn't curse. He went to work and he came home and read the newspaper." In addition, Gladys said he helped shoulder some of the everyday child-rearing responsibilities. "He played with the kids and drove them wherever they needed to go. I didn't always want to drive to some of the faraway places, so he would always drive me or the kids anywhere we needed to go." Asked how having a strong father figure impacted Jerome, Gladys said, "That's all Jerome ever saw: the good things his dad was doing for the family."

Day to day, however, it was about the little things. "We ate dinner together every night, but it was mostly just me and the kids. My husband wasn't there because he had to work. Before he became an electrical inspector, he worked at a steel mill and they worked days, afternoons, and nights." To make up for all that time, the weekends were strictly family time. "We'd go to the park, we'd ride bikes, and my husband built the kids an ice rink in our backyard." Gladys, hardly the type of parent to sit on the side and watch, described how she would roller-skate and play baseball with the three kids. "I just kept the kids extremely active." Active, though, meant more than just physical activity. Gladys said she took Jerome to museums, the library, and even bird-watching.

When it came to religion, Gladys said she wasn't as strict about it as she was about education, meaning the kids didn't have to show up at Sunday school even if they had a fever! "I wasn't a stickler about them going to church every Sunday." Instead she found other, less formal, ways to integrate religion into their lives. "We read the Bible together."

Surprising for someone who is as accomplished a football player as Jerome, Gladys said there wasn't much talk of the sport when he was growing up. "I can't really remember telling him to dream big about becoming a professional football player. I just remember telling him to do the very best that he could. I guess somewhere out of that came his passion for football." It was Gladys's brother, she said, who encouraged her to take Jerome to the next level in his football career. "I remember we were watching Jerome play football and he said, 'You need to do something special with Jerome because Jerome is very smart and a very talented football player. You need to take him out of the Lutheran school and put him into public school where he'll have a better chance of getting a football scholarship to college." While she was a bit resistant to the idea at first, with the lobbying strength of Jerome and his father, Gladys acquiesced, letting him leave the Lutheran school for the local public school. Reflecting on that decision today, Gladys said, "He just really wanted to do it. It wasn't me."

Looking back on where her mothering is most visible in Jerome's life today, Gladys said it's in his charity work. "I took him to community centers and had him talk with kids. It was always my philosophy that he was blessed and therefore was obligated to give back." Jerome has taken his mother's mandate to the next level, going back to visit his old high school to speak about the importance of going to college and involving himself in a plethora of other charitable causes. Gladys said she did more, however, than just tell Jerome to give time: "I'd take him to church and have him stand up and he'd make a speech." But giving orders to Jerome was not how

Gladys parented, nor how she would tell other mothers today to parent. "My main piece of advice would be to always listen to your kids. That is something I always did."

Her other parenting principle was to follow the "no gap" rule. "I worked hard to ensure that my kids wouldn't feel a generation gap with me. In other words, I didn't want them to feel alienated because I was their mother. The rule is really just about staying involved in your kid's lives."

Gladys said parenting has come full circle today. She is now a grandmother to seventeen grandchildren, including Jerome's two children. Describing how she views herself as a parent and a grandparent, Gladys said that, first and foremost, "I'm a teacher. It's amazing I'm seeing my eleven-year-old granddaughter beginning to understand and listen to what I have to say." And that certainly bodes well for her future.

Gloria Allred

Mother of LISA BLOOM

"Children have to have some boundaries, but do not knock the poetry out of the soul."

*G*loria Allred—the mother of Court TV commentator Lisa Bloom—proclaimed that her title is "Proud Mother of Lisa Bloom." It's a name that means a lot more in light of the host of her own accomplishments. Gloria is the most prominent women's rights attorney in the United States. She was rated one of the most important radio talk-show hosts in America by *USA Today* and has won the President's Award from the National Association of Women Lawyers and the 1986 President's Action Award for her work in child support enforcement, presented to her by President Ronald Reagan at the White House. Gloria is also the author of *Fight Back and Win: My Thirty-Year Fight Against Injustice—And How You Can Win Your Own Battles.*

Following in her mother's footsteps, Lisa also became a lawyer and has parlayed her skills onto TV, where she coanchors *Bloom & Politan: Open Court*. Lisa has covered many high-profile justice stories, including the Michael Jackson molestation case, the Scott Peterson murder trial, and the O.J. Simpson case. As a trial lawyer, Lisa's work has set legal precedent on numerous important social issues, including some of the first decisions on the rights of AIDS patients as well as child sexual abuse repressed-memory cases. Lisa has appeared on virtually every major news and magazine program, including *Nightline, Primetime, Today, The Early Show, Larry King Live*, and *Anderson Cooper 360*. She is the author of "Bloom Blog" on CourtTV.com; is a columnist for *Jungle Law Magazine*; has published numerous popular and scholarly articles in *The National Law Journal, NYU Journal of Law and Social Change*, and *Family Circle*; has been featured in many publications, including the *New York Times, TV Guide*, the *Washington Post, Variety*, and the *Hollywood Reporter*; and is profiled in *Who's Who in American Law*. Lisa is active in a number of charities, such as New York Cares, the Achilles Track Club, and the Jewish Home for the Aged. She lives in New York City with her two children.

Growing up in a low-income home, Gloria said, deeply influenced the way she raised her daughter. "I think the fact that I was aware that there are challenges in making a living has always affected me. It made me want to make Lisa a person who would be able to survive on her own and would be able to face life's challenges, which I frankly think are more difficult if you don't have the economic wherewithal in order to face them." As a working mother, Gloria went back to work when Lisa was one year old. "It wasn't easy," Gloria said. "I was bonded, but I felt that since I was a single mother, I needed to finish my education so that I could get a good-paying job. My feeling, which turned out to be correct, was that I was going to be the sole supporter. I wanted to give myself the resources to provide a decent life for her."

It's hardly a surprise that Gloria described Lisa, who would go on to be a National Debate Champion and the Moot Court Champion at Yale Law School, as "very verbal, very articulate, and always surprising everyone." However, all this advanced development did not come at the behest of Gloria. "My outlook was always that the best way to teach reading, or anything for that matter, is to encourage a child to do it for pleasure. . . . I think that children have a natural curiosity and that if you encourage the curiosity they'll want to read, but I don't think it's something that needs to be done on a schedule." It's an approach that certainly worked with Lisa. "I remember when she was younger, we went on a vacation and she couldn't get over the fact that all these children sitting at the pool weren't reading books."

When asked about her mother's parenting technique, Lisa said, "My mom basically stayed out of my way and let me do what I wanted to do," adding the disclaimer of, "you know—as long as it was reasonable." Lisa said this hands-off approach conveyed the enormous confidence her mother had in her abilities. "For example, in school, I always wanted to get straight A's. I generally did, and it wasn't because my mother was bothering me to work hard in school; it was that I was very self-motivated, and I wanted to get good grades. I was competitive and had high aspirations and standards for myself. So, you know, if I had an A- or a B on my report card, I would be embarrassed and my mother would say, 'I mean you can't feel bad about a report card with you know all A's and one A-.' "

Gloria explained that one of her parenting techniques was a conscious effort not to impart *her* fears to Lisa. "I always wanted to be supportive of her . . . for example, I was never a person who did horseback riding or grew up skiing, so I wanted Lisa to be able to explore the things she would like, and take educated risks without fear. . . . Lisa has been able to do a lot of things that I was never able to develop for many reasons, part of which was fear, part of which was economic, part of which was just the lack of time."

As a steward of the law, Gloria said, "I am a big one for the rules. . . . Children have to have some boundaries. . . . It's part of socializing children. I don't believe they can just do or say whatever they want." Still, one has to be careful, as Gloria put it, "not to knock the poetry out of the soul." Gloria said that she has learned that setting parameters about reasonable behavior was not mutually exclusive with expressing oneself. For Gloria, motherhood was also about following through on plans, which, as she put it, "relieved some stress."

Ironically, Gloria initially encouraged Lisa to go to modeling school, something she said she is still in denial about today. "I never actually followed up on it, because I was too busy. I couldn't have been the person who took her there because I was working." Chiming in, Lisa said, "I think the idea was really just to get me into something that I could fall back on and that would also teach me things like what colors looked good on me." Gloria, a master at following her instincts, maintained that Lisa was, and is, a photographer's dream, a fact confirmed by Lisa's TV career. "One may castigate me for all that, but it turns out I was right. I mean, she's not a model, but she's an anchor."

When reflecting on her mother's parenting style, Lisa discussed the confidence her mother had in her judgment. Explaining her philosophy, Gloria said, "It was always my belief that you need to give children information and education and help them think about what choices they should be making and what the consequences are for those choices and what the benefits are and what the risks are." It's an approach that is rippling down the generations. "I want to instill that same confidence in my children," Lisa said. "The goal, as my mother taught me, is not to have carbon copies of me. The goal is for them to be independent, self-sufficient people with good judgment who can go off into the world and make good choices. To that end, you have to let them start making little choices for themselves as soon as possible, and then as they get older, you let them make bigger and bigger choices."

When Lisa was a teenager, Gloria recalled that she wanted to have a later curfew. "I said that you have to go to Planned Parenthood. They had a special class for teenagers about birth control and reproductive issues. I just wanted her to have all the information so she could make the best choices possible." Lisa is now having the same conversation with her daughter. "Last weekend, I had a long discussion about birth control with my daughter and some of her seventeen-year-old friends. I was given a lot of information as a teenager, and I want to give my daughter the same knowledge advantage. . . . It's my belief that with teenagers, if you give them the right information, they are going to make good choices."

While Gloria was far from a nag, she did encourage Lisa's academic pursuits. Lisa now endearingly refers to her mother as "my publicist." Looking back, Gloria said, "I always encouraged Lisa to talk about important issues, to ask questions, and debate things. I encourage that in my grandchildren as well." Gloria felt this was a way to foster Lisa's innate talents. "I think that's the key to helping a child be successful—help them to recognize their strengths and help them to minimize their weaknesses." Gloria also conveyed an evolved understanding that the umbilical cord was cut at birth. "Parenting is also about recognizing that they're not going to be you. They're going to be their own human being." Gloria also parented (and grandparents) with brutal honesty. "Maybe it's a good thing or maybe it's not, but my grandchildren know I won't tell them it's great unless I really think it is."

Gloria called Lisa "a designer child." Expanding on that, Gloria said, "She doesn't just talk the talk, she walks the walk"—a walk that is definitely part her mother's strut. "I always told her that if you are going to invest your time, it is more important to invest it for social change than invest it for service. In other words, it's the difference between working to stop a war and bandaging those who have been wounded in the war. If you can stop the war, there won't be any need in the future to bandage those who have been wounded in the war."

Lisa said this philosophy had a profound impact on her and has shaped her own career trajectory. "My mother took me to Equal Rights Amendment rallies, gay rights marches, and union organizing events. She definitely always exposed me to the concept of social change, and that it is important to work for social change and not bandage things one by one." Above all, Gloria said, "Child rearing is about showing children that it is our duty to help others in the community"—a value that Lisa certainly carries in her DNA and manifests in her daily life.

Using a gardening metaphor, Gloria said parenting is similar to watching a flower grow into something beautiful. Likening a parent to the sunshine, she said, "The sunshine is positive reinforcement to the flower and the support that gives the flower strength to bloom. The flower, though, will be what the flower is meant to be. You, as a parent, just have to be the proper support for the flower, in order for it to reach its potential."

Helen Bolotin

Mother of MICHAEL BOLTON

"Whatever they did I hoped they could tell me. It was more important that I try to understand them, even if I didn't agree with them."

Helen Bolotin, mother of Michael Bolton—one of the most successful musicians in the industry—said that, when they were growing up, her children used to call her a "mommy hippie." Her parenting approach might have been unconventional, but it certainly hasn't hindered her son from reaching the top of his field. Born in New Haven, Connecticut, Michael found his biggest success in his midthirties and early forties as a solo vocalist in the adult contemporary/easy listening genre. He has written chart-topping songs for artists including Barbra Streisand, Kiss, Kenny Rogers, Kenny G, and Patti LaBelle. In 1993, he established the Michael Bolton Foundation to assist women and children at risk from the effects of poverty and emotional, physical, and sexual abuse. Michael has three daughters.

Growing up, Helen said she had the most wonderful parents anyone could have asked for. "My parents were the best parents. . . . We had a very lively household and there was always music playing." Carrying this model of a close-knit family over to the next generation, Helen said, Michael and his brother, Orrin, were very close with their grandfather, Helen's father. "We visited their grandparents a great deal, and my mom would often come babysit on the weekends."

As Helen described Michael's upbringing, the path from childhood to stardom seemed like a logical progression. "The children were always listening to music at home," Helen said. "As [babies] the three of them sang, and we would all sing together as a family."

While Helen described her parents as the best parents in the world, in her own parenting approach she deviated from how she was raised. "Everyone said I was too lenient with my children, and I suppose it was because my parents wouldn't allow me to do certain things." Still, many parts of Michael's upbringing were very "by the book." "We ate dinner together every night . . . we would go bowling with the children, the boys played Little League." However, as Michael got older, Helen said it was difficult to keep him on a schedule. "He played in clubs and would come home at three A.M. and eat dinner," Helen recalled about Michael's early years as a performer.

When presented with a choice, Helen emphasized fairness over leniency. "The children knew I was fair, or tried to be." Above all, Helen highlighted the joy that permeated their household. "We all just had a great time together." Looking back today, however, Helen said that a lot of the other mothers didn't always approve of what she viewed as "fun." Conveying a certain confidence in her out-of-the-box parenting style, she said, "My parenting approach worked for me and for my children . . . and I did have some moms who actually thanked me for my advice!"

Helen's home was always the social hub. "The kids all came to our house. My house was really the center of my three children's friends. . . . I had fun having them there. . . . Some mothers would call me and ask me what their child was doing and I used to say, 'Having fun.'" Helen said she took playing with her kids to the next level. "I became their ages a lot. We had a great time together. . . . I was a very affectionate mother."

Asked about what she did specifically to help Michael get where he is today, Helen said, "I just always told him to find what he loved to do and stick with it. I also emphasized that he had to do something that he truly believed in and wanted to work hard on." But she pushed harder for Michael to become a ballplayer than a musician. "Michael didn't get into music until he was singing at a church and this gentleman was there and asked me, 'Where did he get that voice?' I told him, stupidly, 'I don't have a clue.' It was after that he finally got some training." Religion played a bigger role in Michael's life. "We were a family that believed in God," Helen said. However, she didn't try to force it down their throats. "I allowed my children all of the freedom they needed and prayed a lot!"

Keeping the channels of communication open was also central to Helen's parenting approach. Circling back to her leniency, Helen said, "I was not a strict mom because I wanted them to know that I loved them so very much and whatever they did I hoped they could tell me. It was more important that I try to understand them, even if I didn't agree with them." It was Helen's belief that childhood was a time to explore things—safely. "I always encouraged the children in whatever they wanted to do as long as it was a learning process."

But like any mother, Helen said she told Michael to be careful, while always imparting the deep sense of trust she had in her son's ability to make good decisions. "Michael would often go play in places that I was concerned about, but trust is just so important and I wanted him to know that I felt he was smart and knew how to stay out of trouble."

Helen credited her laid-back, open-minded approach for helping Michael get where he is today. "I didn't shelter Michael from the world. I think he is so intelligent because of all the wonderful places he has been exposed to." For Helen, the proof is tangible. Michael dedicated his CD *Till the End of Time* to his mother.

Helen's advice to mothers about how to instill the principle of success is: "I would say to encourage a child in whatever he or she is interested in. I think it's so important to listen to the child and not feel like so many parents who think, 'Next year, he or she will be interested in something else.' It's just so important to really listen. I did, and look what happened."

Roberta Shields

Mother of CHRISTOPHER BRIDGES AKA LUDACRIS

"Your fears don't necessarily have to become your child's fears."

$\mathcal{R}$oberta Shields—the mother of Christopher Bridges, known to music fans as Ludacris—said her big piece of advice to mothers is: learn from your child because they have so much to teach you. She is the president of his foundation and the chief operating officer for business enterprises at Chris's company—ventures that include real-estate holdings and aviation.

In 1999, Chris released his first independent album, *Incognegro*, which sold more than fifty thousand copies. A year later, in 2000, Chris was signed to Def Jam Recordings and released his major label debut, *Back for the First Time*. Chris has also collaborated and toured with several hip-hop stars, including Missy Elliott, 50 Cent, Busta Rhymes, and Eminem. In December 2001, Chris cofounded the Ludacris Foundation, a nonprofit organization to help youngsters achieve their dreams. Chris has guest-starred on *Law & Order: Special Victims Unit*, *Saturday Night Live*, *Late Night with Conan O'Brien*, *The Tonight Show with Jay Leno*, *The Late Show with David Letterman*, *The Oprah Winfrey Show*, *Jimmy Kimmel Live! Total Request Live*, and *The Daily Show*. Chris also starred in *The Fast and the Furious*, *Hustle N' Flow*, and the Oscar-winning film *Crash*. *Teen People* named Chris one of the "25 Hottest Stars Under 25" in 2002. His musical acclaim was recognized with a Grammy Award in 2005 with Usher and Lil Jon for their hit single "Yeah," as well as in 2007 for Best Rap Album, *Release Therapy*, and Best Rap Song, "Money Maker." Chris is the proud father of one daughter.

For Roberta, parenting was all about "walking the walk and talking the talk. . . . It's about showing consistency in what you're asking them to do and what you're requiring of yourself. You really have to value their thoughts, their feelings, and then it will be reciprocated." In practice, this often meant that Roberta gave her son the opportunity to share his thoughts before jumping to conclusions. "I would always try to ask open-ended questions, rather than accusatory ones like, 'What happened here?' 'Did you do this?' Instead, I would say, 'Tell me a little about what was going on before I got here.' "

Roberta said her parenting style was about showing Chris that success was as much about tenacity as it was about achievement. "My father instilled in me that failure is not about falling down, it's about getting up, so I believe it's very important to take risks." Roberta recalled one of the most valuable parenting lessons she learned was that parents need to let their children test their wings and make their own mistakes. "When Chris was six years old he came and said, 'Mom, I'm going to win this contest.' I kept thinking, 'How am I going to prepare him for loss?' Then he came on that fourth day and said, 'You know what, Mom? Mandy's got a good idea, too. She just might win.' I learned that your fears don't necessarily have to become your child's fears."

It was this evolved understanding of Chris as a *separate* person that Roberta said allowed him to cultivate the self-assurance that got him where he is today, literally at the top of the charts. "I had the confidence that he would figure it out. I think sometimes parents want to prepare their child for hurt. I think, too, being African-American, you want to prepare your kids for some of those ugly situations, but I've learned to hang back and make sure I'm listening, because my experience might not be his experience."

Goals and dreams were hardly some abstraction for Roberta. "We would always talk about goals and objectives, and ever since Chris was eight years old, until his sophomore year in college, he wrote down his goals for the year." Roberta said this exercise certainly paid off, particularly as Chris got older. "He became disciplined and very goal oriented. He had a plan. A lot of young people want something and don't know how to get it. They don't identify the steps, but Chris learned how to do that early on."

Helping Chris identify the steps to take him where he wanted to go was how Roberta saw her role as a mother. "Instead of just vaguely encouraging him to be a musician, I would say, 'Are you taking music lessons now?' . . . I encouraged and supported him in getting involved in activities that leveraged and strengthened his talents." Roberta credited this approach, among other things, with getting Chris where he is today. "He was so focused on his music and he ended up collecting friends who also had a similar type of focus." And that was no accident.

Like any mother of a teenager, Roberta quickly picked up on the importance friends play in a child's life. Roberta said she deeply internalized something the principal of Chris's school once said: "The people who have the most influence on your child's life are his friends." Adopting those words of wisdom, Roberta made a genuine effort to get to know her son's friends. "Every month, I would treat them all to brunch. We would talk about their interests and what was going on in their lives." Recalling that time, Roberta said, "I think I understood, and imparted to Chris, the importance of what your friends bring to the table. There are friends who are going to help you realize your goals and dreams. Those are the people who are willing to help you along the way." In fact, it was a moment with his friends that Roberta said was the crystallizing one for her about her son's future success. "I remember I went to the studio with Chris when he was eleven years old with his friends. I realized, then, that my son was an artist and producer who was deeply committed to music and was really going to go places."

A successful businesswoman at Freddie Mac, a Fortune 100 company, Roberta credited herself as a good developer of others' talents. "Even when I had a staff of people, I was the one who had the highest percentage of them that would get promotions. I think I'm a motivator. But more than that, I teach people to be motivated from within." That's why *developer*, Roberta said, is a word that better describes her than *mom*. "I think parenting is really about development, motivation, and helping people realize that whoever has the most to win and the most to lose is the one that's most responsible—and that's you."

It's hardly a surprise, and some might even say inevitable, that Chris has dedicated so much of his life to philanthropy. Describing a lineage that made giving back the focus of their lives, Roberta said, "My grandmother had a store, and if people couldn't afford to buy things, she would give them credit, or they'd bring a bushel of corn the next time. But it was the idea that if you were in the position to do that, then you should. Today, I see that Chris's whole team is like that. The foundation was founded on giving young people opportunities." Roberta said that even if Chris didn't have all that he has, he would still be just as charitable as he is today. "The money has just allowed him to take it to the next level."

Roberta also attributes Chris's choices and accomplishments to the role religion played in his life. "We were very religious. We attended church on Sunday and religion was part of our daily life."

She credited her own religious upbringing, saying "My parents instilled in us family values, including the importance of God, moral values, and the strong belief in the value of education. I was always told, 'A weak mind makes a weak man.'"

Roberta said she had fluid definitions of success and achievement. "I always expected Chris to do his best. I would say, 'get that A,' but I also let him know I would take a hard-earned 'C' over an easy 'A' any day." Still, that hardly meant that Roberta accepted mediocrity. "Just as my parents told me, I told Chris, 'We are not average, and I expect you to perform above average.'" However, personal growth and development were always more important to her than grades. "I would encourage Chris to ask questions, get the facts, and then I would tell him to make his decisions." Outlining her three-step approach, Roberta said, "I would encourage, understand, and then tell him to take a risk." Above all, her goal was to nurture personal responsibility. "Of course I wanted Chris to understand what others' expectations of him were, but I wanted him to know his *own* expectations and let those guide him."

Distilling the essence of all the wisdom that she passed on to her son, Roberta said it was about telling Chris to "Visualize it and then realize it. . . . I also always told him to love what you do and do what you love." As a mother who placed such a high value on independence, Roberta certainly doesn't take all the credit. "Chris is responsible for shaping his future and living his dreams." However, Roberta does see her role somewhere in the big picture. "I think that a child who is loved, supported, and grows up in fertile ground will have a lot greater chance of becoming successful." Asked to describe herself in a sentence, Roberta captured the soul of her mothering style when she said, "The image I have of myself as a parent is: guardian, teacher, mentor, and a mother who holds her son accountable for shaping his own future."

Marge Brinkley
Mother of CHRISTIE BRINKLEY

"Explore life on your terms, with humor and humility, and do not be afraid of failure."

*M*arge Brinkley—mother of supermodel, writer, photographer, actress, and celebrity mom Christie Brinkley—said that she taught Christie that life is a celebration. "I told her to explore life on your terms, with humor and humility, and do not be afraid of failure." Internalizing these wise words from her mother has helped Christie become the Renaissance woman she is today. In addition to having been featured on more than five hundred magazine covers in both the United States and Europe, Christie broke records with her *Sports Illustrated* "Christie Brinkley Calendar," has made guest appearances on just about every TV talk show, and has held major contracts with CoverGirl, MasterCard, and Diet Coke. She has also illustrated and written a bestselling book, painted the cover for Billy Joel's platinum album *River of Dreams*, and been the in-ring photographer for many of Don King's boxing matches. Proving that she is much more than "a pretty face," Christie is also actively involved in the March of Dimes and the Make-a-Wish Foundation and is the mother of three children.

In describing her parenting style, Marge emphasized how much she trusted Christie. Even as a young adult, Marge made cultivating Christie's independence—the independence that would be crucial to Christie's achievements—a priority. "When Christie was eighteen years old, she wanted desperately to move to Paris. After much soul searching, Don and I bit the bullet and gave our approval . . . an act of trust that scared us to death. But it worked out beautifully. Christie moved to Paris, where she lived, studied, and worked for eight joyously productive years." It was while working in Paris as a professional illustrator that Christie was "discovered" by a photographer.

Before being discovered, Christie grew up in Malibu, California, with her parents and older brother, Greg. A strong, close-knit family was a critical component of Christie's upbringing. Marge said the family would gather for dinner every night around their cozy dining table, "laughing and swapping stories about our most recent adventures." In addition to this nightly ritual, Marge said, "When they least expected it, we would surprise the kids by whisking them away for a weekend in San Francisco or Mexico. We were always traveling as a loving family unit."

Marge stressed that she let Christie develop at her own pace. "Christie walked at nine months, talked in complete sentences at one year." When it came to reading, Marge prodded a little more. "We read to our kids every day at naptime and bedtime. We encouraged them to have a healthy respect for books." The other area where Marge pushed was when it came to physical activity. "Today, thanks to my prodding (or nagging), she is a Class A swimmer, an excellent skier, a competitive-level tennis player, an enthusiastic rock climber, and she's good at hopscotch, too."

Television was the area where Marge said she was the strictest. "My husband was—and is—an award-winning writer-producer for TV, so the kids had a unique perspective on television. We were extremely selective regarding the shows they were allowed to watch." But in terms of other forms of entertainment, such as music, Marge was much more liberal. "Music was an important factor in the lives of our kids. We made a point to expose them to every genre, from jazz to folk to classical."

In line with her general parenting philosophy of letting Christie find her own way, Marge said she never imposed control over Christie's playtime. "I believe that play is a form of creativity, and as such, it should not be heavily structured." Growing up, Christie was extremely social. "Her friends spent most of their after-school hours at our house, baking cookies, making puddings, generally messing up the kitchen. I made sure all the ingredients were available, and they did the rest." It was the little things, such as just being there with baking ingredients when Christie got home from school, or attending every open house at the school and the informal meetings with teachers, that Marge believes were the critical components of her day-to-day parenting style.

Marge's main focus was Christie's development as a *human being*, rather than setting professional expectations for her daughter. "I was more concerned with how she would face the world with honesty, trust, self-respect, and humor." To nurture this goal, Marge said she wasn't the type of parent who would clap when Christie got out of bed in the morning. In fact, Marge said she modulated her accolades. "To encourage honesty, trust, and self-respect, I praised Christie only when it was absolutely called for, which was impressively frequent because she was so damned remarkable." When it came to discipline, Marge said that she and her husband were only strict when it concerned values. "We made a point to be consistent in our judgments, and our kids respected us for it."

Also, instead of just giving praise, Marge and her husband

always tried to *do* things to actively encourage Christie to develop her talents. "We always felt that Christie had special gifts for painting, music, and languages." To encourage her pursuit of these talents, Marge said they had Christie's artwork professionally framed and displayed throughout their homes. "Her talents motivated us to enroll her in Le Lycée Français and sponsor all those trips to Europe. Today, she's at home anywhere in the world and speaks five languages."

While religion played a "moderate" role in how Marge raised Christie—the Brinkleys didn't subscribe to conventionally organized religion—she taught the kids that "God was in our hearts, our minds, and in our love for each other."

Marge described Christie as someone who always dreams big and enjoys the process of turning dreams into reality. "When she needed guidance, she knew she could depend on me to help her." It was this hands-off, and slightly out-of-the-box, parenting style that contributed to Christie's enormous accomplishments. As she reflected on Christie's success today, Marge said, "Christie had a firm desire to treat life as a celebration. As far as I can see, she is still celebrating." For Marge, the confirmation of her parenting skills comes from the incredibly close relationship she has with Christie today. "If I measure the love and respect I receive from my children, I know that I've been a wonderful parent."

Sandra Cain

Mother of BOBBI BROWN

"Nurture them when they are upset."

*S*andra Cain, mother of Bobbi Brown—the renowned makeup artist and founder of Bobbi Brown Cosmetics—said she always knew there was something special about Bobbi. "She definitely had a creative streak. Bobbi was always singing and dancing around, and she loved using my old makeup to make up her dolls and herself." Little did Sandra know that Bobbi would turn this "creative streak" into a product line that is sold in more than four hundred stores and twenty countries worldwide. Bobbi started her makeup revolution in 1991 with a handful of lipsticks and a simple philosophy: "Women want to look and feel like themselves, only prettier and more confident." Her dream was realized when she debuted her line of cosmetics—just ten brown-based lipsticks—at Bergdorf Goodman in New York City.

Bobbi has also forged her place as one of the leading beauty experts in the field, dispensing advice and taking audiences through her signature makeup how-tos on television programs like *Today*, *The View*, and *The Oprah Winfrey Show*. You can also find her backstage at the fashion shows in New York City, creating runway makeup looks for designers ranging from Badgley Mischka to Matthew Williamson and Red Dress "Heart Truth." Equally adept with a pen as she is with a makeup brush, Bobbi has written *New York Times*–bestselling books and advice columns for her customers—from teens to their grandmothers. Bobbi's most recent book, a *New York Times* bestseller, *Bobbi Brown Living Beauty*, was published in the spring of 2007. She is also involved in charities such as Jane Addams Vocational High School and Dress for Success, which help to empower underprivileged young girls and women. Bobbi is married and the mother of three sons.

Reflecting on her own upbringing, Sandra said that coming from an upper-middle-class family affected the way she raised Bobbi, bringing a sense of tenacity and drive to her parenting style. "I wanted her to have the same—if not better—opportunities and things than I had." To give her that, Sandra worked through her pregnancy as a secretary at her father's business. "I took two and a half weeks off before I had Bobbi and was on maternity leave for about two and a half months. I eventually had to go back to work because my father was losing his business and needed my help." Like so many parents today, Sandra did the ubiquitous juggling act. "I would get up at 6 A.M. to feed Bobbi, prepare breakfast for my husband, then I would drive my husband to school and Bobbi to my mother's house, and get to work by 9 A.M."

Sandra said that Bobbi hit certain milestones on time but was a late walker, which worried her. "Bobbi was about nine months old when she started to crawl. . . . She talked at about twelve months. . . . She didn't walk until she was fourteen months old. When I asked her doctors about it, they told me not to worry. They told me to hold her hand to help her when she tried to walk." This became a metaphor for their relationship, as Sandra would hold

Bobbi's hand—more figuratively later in life—to help her overcome certain hurdles and obstacles.

Reading was an important ritual and bonding activity for Bobbi and her mother. "I read to Bobbi as much as I could before bedtime. Her favorites were the Disney books, and all the classic nursery rhymes." Sandra took Bobbi to puppet theaters to expose her to different kinds of music. "Bobbi loved nursery rhymes. She started singing the songs on her own when she was about two and even knew how to sing all the melodies." It was an approach of *doing* things together that Sandra took with Bobbi, even when it came to informal playtime. "Sometimes I initiated games. . . . We'd sit on the floor with a ball and roll it back and forth. When Bobbi got older, she loved playing jacks, pickup sticks, Shoots and Ladders, and Monopoly."

Sandra described a laid-back style when it came to planning Bobbi's extracurricular activities. "When Bobbi was young we had a jungle gym and merry-go-round in the backyard. Her friends from the neighborhood would come over and they'd spend the afternoon playing outdoors." Even when Sandra did enroll Bobbi in actual lessons, there was no pressure. "I enrolled Bobbi in ballet when she was about nine years old, but she quit when the teacher asked her to dance the part of Cinderella for a televised performance."

Sandra said that she encouraged Bobbi in very specific areas. "I encouraged Bobbi to be social and she had a lot of friends in the neighborhood. She always got along well with others." Bobbi was a good student, so Sandra didn't have to push her to get good grades. "She was driven and had her own high standards. She always came home with an exceptional report card. The only thing I told her was to make something of her life." However, Sandra didn't coddle Bobbi; instead, she tried to instill in Bobbi a "get back on the horse" attitude. "I tried to nurture her when she was upset. . . . After a little encouragement I'd send her back out to take another stab at whatever it was that was challenging her." This lesson helped Bobbi enormously in an industry that is hardly for the meek.

Sandra said, "I was always very involved. I was the parent who went to school to check on the kids' grades and talk to their teachers." She also went to her children's school to help out in the lunchroom, "which used to embarrass the kids because I'd tell them to behave."

Sandra and her husband separated after fifteen years of marriage, but she said there was still a sense of normalcy, even as the kids shuttled between two homes. "We ate together nearly every night on school nights. The kids alternated weekends with me and their father. When they were with me, we spent a lot of time hanging out in the backyard, swimming and barbecuing." Sandra attributed her ability to keep the family so intact after the divorce to the great relationship her kids had with her new husband, Norty. "We were lucky to have a very solid family unit. . . . The kids had a good relationship with Norty."

As Bobbi got older, and the nature of their relationship changed, Sandra saw her role as a sounding board to help Bobbi work through things when she was unhappy. "When Bobbi was in college she went through a phase where she was considering dropping out. She didn't like the fact that everyone partied so much, and she didn't like her classes. I asked her what she would do if it was her birthday and she could do anything she wanted to do. She said she wanted to play with makeup. After doing some research, she decided to go to Emerson College in Boston."

For Sandra, cultivating an open channel of communication with Bobbi was a critical component of her parenting style, and one that helped Bobbi realize, and actualize, her goals. "She called me once because she wasn't comfortable with an upcoming job that involved putting body makeup on girls in bikinis and men in jockstraps. I told her to pretend that they were mannequins and that helped her."

Sandra's parenting credo was about helping Bobbi find her interests and encouraging her to pursue them. Even so, Sandra said that in her wildest dreams she never thought that Bobbi would be as famous as she is. "I often just said to her, 'Keep up the good work, honey.' I also told her to go for her heart's desire and things would fall into place."

Barbara Bush

Mother of PRESIDENT GEORGE W. BUSH AND JEB BUSH

"Success is a person who is happy in what they do,
thoughtful of others, who helps others and shares."

*B*arbara Bush, one of the most revered women in America,
said that she never thought she was a great mother. However, as the mother of five übersuccessful children, she
clearly did something right. Her most notable son is George W.
Bush, the former governor of Texas and now the two-term forty-
third president of the United States. Her other children include the
wildly popular two-term governor of Florida, Jeb; two successful
businessmen, Neil and Marvin; and a daughter, Dorothy, who has
devoted her life to philanthropic work. All five children are married with children of their own.

When Barbara was a young mother of twenty-one, she suffered
an early tragedy when her second child, Robin, died of leukemia
before her fourth birthday. "Her death influenced all the other five,
although only George W. knew her." Using that experience as a
source of compassion, Barbara said that "Because of Robin, George

and I love every living human more." Seeing compassion modeled for him, it's no coincidence that George W. formed his own political platform around "compassionate conservatism."

Reflecting on her parenting approach, Barbara said it was as simple as "unconditional love and enthusiastic encouragement." Viewing life, and particularly her family, through a religious lens, Barbara said, "As parents we were aware of what a blessing our children were." For the Bush family, religion was a central part of their lives, and a value that has certainly shaped George W.'s character and political career. Barbara said, "Religion was a great help to us, although I would say that our household was moderately religious. . . . We went to church every Sunday and there was no question that we all went with some moaning on the children's part sometimes." Barbara explained that religion was also incorporated into their day-to-day routines. "We ate together as a family, as did both our families when we were growing up, and said grace before meals."

The importance of just being together was paramount in the Bush family. Whether it was carrying on the tradition of visiting the Bush-Walker grandparents at Walker's Point every summer, just as George Bush Sr. had done, or eating together every night, family was the focal point for the Bush household. "Our children grew up with a huge group of extended family who were always there for them," Barbara said. With five kids to wrangle, Barbara said she had help during the week from the time her second child, Robin, was born. "The same lady from Mexico moved in with us forty-six years ago and still lives with us."

When it came to encouraging her children to explore directions for their careers, Barbara said she didn't pressure them toward politics, although it was certainly in the forefront of their lives. During his forty-four-year political career, George Bush Sr. served as a member of Congress, U.S. ambassador to the United Nations, chairman of the Republican National Committee, director of the

CIA, and finally as vice president and president of the United States. Barbara said, "We told them [the children] they could be anything they wanted to be." Barbara also modeled *her* idea of success, and public service, for the children. "To me, success is a person who is happy in what they do, thoughtful of others, who helps others and shares." It's a logical progression that two of her children are public servants and one has devoted her life to full-time charity work.

Where Barbara said she did more active encouraging was when it came to reading. Literacy has been Barbara's pet cause, and Barbara read to the children every night before they went to bed. When it came to extracurricular activities, she encouraged George W. and the other three boys to play sports, but made sure it was all "just for fun." "They exercised a lot and raced around the neighborhood with friends." However, the Bush household was anything but a free-for-all. Barbara described the Bush home life "as a scheduled one." "They had bedtimes, and after a book reading, either by their father or me, if they were young, lights out."

When it came to expectations, Barbara said, "All five children knew their dad and I expected them to do well in school and in their relationships with others. They really tried to win their dad's and my approval." Barbara also described her desire to cultivate a sense of independence for her children. "They were made to do their homework and we did not help them unless they asked."

Barbara ran a tight ship—a management approach that George W. has brought to the White House—running short, to-the-point meetings. "When we moved from Midland, Texas, to Houston, I had a whistle I blew for mealtimes if they were playing in the neighborhood. . . . Like my mother I was the enforcer and their dad was the favorite."

In addition to being the "enforcer," Barbara was the linchpin, and stabilizer, for a family always on the move. The Bush family moved twenty-nine times during her husband's almost half-century political career. Barbara said she always tried to keep strong roots

Martha Cherry

Mother of MARC CHERRY

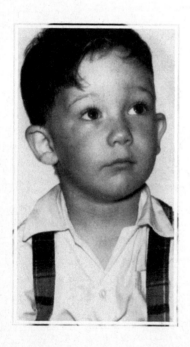

"Envy is a wasted effort. There's always going to be someone who is better looking, has more money, and is smarter, so pick out the talent that you're good at and the others will fall in place."

*M*artha Cherry, the mother of *Desperate Housewives* creator Marc Cherry, said that the character Bree is loosely based on her. She explained, "Well, see, we are both always pushing manners and encouraging people to be socially correct." Marc began his career as a personal assistant on *Designing Women*, and in 1990 he became a writer and producer for the hit sitcom *The Golden Girls*. Marc then went on to create the sitcom *The Five Mrs. Buchanans* in 1994 and later worked on other series such as *The Crew* in 1995 and *Some of My Best Friends* in 2001. In 2004, ABC picked up his series *Desperate Housewives*. The show was an immediate success and is consistently rated one of the top two programs among viewers in the United States. *Desperate Housewives* has won the Screen Actors Guild Award, The People's Choice Award, a Golden

Globe, and Emmy awards. Marc was recently honored by the Log Cabin Republicans, a gay political group. He's also active in the Los Angeles Gay and Lesbian Center.

As the oldest of three children, Martha said she was the most uptight with Marc. "There came a time, pretty quickly, however, when I realized I was overdoing it." Describing a typical childhood, Martha said, "I read all the nursery rhymes, and we had a children's Bible, and I had a big easy chair. I'd put the baby in my lap and I'd put the other two on the armchair and I would read the stories of the Bible to them." When Marc was three, Martha intuited that he needed more outside activity, so she enrolled him in day care. Looking back on Marc's childhood, Martha described having a strong support system in her close-knit group of friends. "We were all having children at around the same time and our children grew up playing together. We have maintained those relationships for years." Martha encouraged her house to be the social epicenter for all the children in her neighborhood. "I remember Marc once asked if it bothered me to have so many kids around and I said, 'Absolutely not, because then I know who you are with.' "

Reflecting on her parenting approach, Martha explained that pressure was not her style. "I told Marc whatever he did was his choice. . . . I believe that everyone has a talent, so I told him to pick out the thing he was good at and the other stuff will fall into place." This was all coupled with praise and encouragement. "I did not believe in ever putting Marc down about anything. The goal of a parent is to build self-esteem." Surprisingly, in light of her son's career path, Martha said she wasn't a TV watcher, and consequently neither were the children. "I was just too busy during the day," she said. "I never watched soap operas. I thought they had their problems, and I had mine. They'd take of theirs and I'd take of mine."

Like most tight-knit families, the Cherrys spent weekends together. "We would go to the movies, we would take the kids out to breakfast after church, and we went out to dinner during the week.

When Marc got older, he was in Little League and I saw to it that he had tennis lessons. Marc also came everywhere with us." Even though Bree, the strictest of the desperate housewives, is loosely based on Martha, she said she was much more laid-back. "I didn't try to control every move. That would have been impossible with three children. I tried to keep them from fighting. . . . Marc and Meghan, my daughter, are always saying that my favorite expression was, 'Let's not be unpleasant.'" Martha said she also imparted valuable wisdom passed down from her mother. "I always told Marc something my mother told me. She said, 'Envy is a wasted effort. There's always going to be someone who is better looking, has more money, and is smarter, so pick out the talent that you're good at and the others will fall in place.'"

Further evidence that Martha was hardly a desperate housewife is her experience living abroad in Hong Kong and Iran, locations the family moved to because of her husband's job. Reflecting on her experience living there with an eleven-, twelve-, and thirteen-year-old, Martha said, "In Iran, I was the first woman to drive a car with the company. I wanted to be able to drive the kids to their swim practice." In addition to the cultural exposure that just living in places as different as Hong Kong and Iran gave Marc, Martha supplemented these experiences with museum visits and other activities. "It was never a forced thing," she said. "We didn't go every day. But there were always books at our house. In fact, our houses were always loaded with books." Martha said Marc gravitated toward mystery books the most growing up, so it's not surprising that *Desperate Housewives* has a mystery component to its plot.

When it came to school, Martha said she didn't push Marc. "We always made sure that the homework was done and there was a lot of praise for anything he did well." She was always careful not to stifle Marc's creative streak, even when he wrote stories that were a little dark. "When he was ten years old, he wrote a story about how my husband and I poisoned each other. . . . I just thought it was pretty funny. That's another thing; my husband had a wonderful sense of humor. I have a pretty good one, we always just kind of laughed. We just didn't take anything too seriously." As a corollary, Martha said, "I never lost faith in Marc. I just believed whatever happened was a bump in the road and things would go on."

When she was asked what advice she would give other mothers about tapping into their child's creativity, Martha said, "Every child has a talent, whether it's sports, art, or music. You just have to let them express themselves in the way that is unique to them." For Martha that sometimes meant encouraging Marc's morbid stories. Martha sees her role as a mother captured by the image of a little bird being groomed for bigger things. "You teach it how to fly, and you let it fly. I think overcontrolling is terrible. I think that is stifling, rather than stimulating. I think you do need to discipline because it teaches self-discipline, but you also have to be stable. I've always tried to be stable." Last but not least, Martha said, "I think manners are important," something Bree Van De Kamp would certainly agree with.

Gladys Clash

Mother of ELMO CREATOR KEVIN CLASH

"Everything in life is not going to be the way you want it to be."

*G*ladys Clash, the mother of Kevin Clash—the creator of Elmo, the beloved *Sesame Street* character—said that when Kevin was growing up, because he was so good at sports, people used to ask, " 'Why doesn't he go outside and play ball more?' But I saw that he had a talent, which was drawing and creating, so I nurtured it." Kevin started building his puppet empire when he was growing up, making puppets in his bedroom. His incredible talent then catapulted him to *Captain Kangaroo,* and then to *Sesame Street,* where he has brought his furry red friend, Elmo, into millions of homes.

Nominated several times for an Emmy, Kevin took home the award in 1990 for outstanding performer in a children's series. He won again in 2001 for his work as coexecutive producer of *Sesame*

Street. Kevin also recently published his book *My Life as a Furry Red Monster: What Being Elmo Has Taught Me About Life, Love and Laughing Out Loud.* Kevin has a nine-year-old daughter, Shannon Elyse Clash.

Raised as one of four children right outside Baltimore, Gladys said she ran a tight ship. "I was strict in a way where I would tell them right from wrong, but not in a way that would hinder them. . . . But I stuck to my guns, even if my kids were mad or angry." Although Gladys classified their socioeconomic status as poor, that was hardly a representation of life in the Clash household, which Gladys described as quite vibrant. "We had a very happy home life. The kids were not denied anything. I took them to theaters. . . . We didn't have a big house, but the rooms were colorful. Kevin had drawn rocket ships on the walls."

As a child, Kevin was surrounded by other children—not just his brothers and sisters. "I worked in day care," Gladys said. "I had nine kids I was taking care of in addition to Kevin. We would all sing songs and listen to music like Frank Sinatra." Reflecting back on her decision to be responsible for all these kids in addition to her own, Gladys explained, "I just loved to work with kids."

Gladys said she was pretty liberal about the amount of television she let Kevin watch, a parenting choice that has certainly paid its dividends. "I let Kevin watch TV shows like *Nancy's Romper Room*. TV was really different from what it is now." In fact, Kevin credits having been a *Sesame Street* fan from early childhood as part of his inspiration for creating Elmo. Growing up, however, Gladys saw Kevin's creative streak manifest in an understated way. "Kevin was always a quiet person." Although he did all the "normal" childhood activities, such as play ball, he was, as Gladys put it, "a deep child." "He was very creative, always drawing and inventing things," she said.

Gladys saw that from an early age Kevin had an arsenal of creative talents. She was careful, however, not to overwhelm him. "I made sure it was something that *he* wanted to do. I saw how some parents push their kids and make them do things that they don't want to do." Using this approach, Gladys said, "We helped Kevin as much as possible. We supported him in everything he did." Kevin wasn't very good at reading, so she worked with him to find a way to make the daunting task more surmountable. "I came up with the idea that Kevin should read *TV Guide,* and that really helped him."

In addition, Gladys offered up words of encouragement, framing them in the context of Kevin's bigger dreams and aspirations. "I told him that it was very important that he be fluent in math and reading. I said to him, 'Kevin, you have to learn these things so when you become a famous puppeteer, you'll know what to do with your money.'" But Gladys's parenting style was not about talking *at* Kevin. "To me, my parenting style was about letting Kevin talk to me. It was letting him tell me how we were raising him. It was more about communicating." Her method had great results—through Elmo, Kevin communicates with and charms adults and children every day.

Growing up male in a predominately African-American community made Kevin's career choice and creative interests all the more unusual. "I remember the kids in the neighborhood would sometimes tease him for not wanting to come out and play ball," Gladys recalled. "I told him not to worry about what people say about you." Gladys's mantra to Kevin was, "'As long as you are happy with what you are doing, we will support you one hundred percent.'" Giving Kevin all the support and love that she did, Gladys said, was augmented by her marriage to her husband, with whom she celebrated her fifty-second wedding anniversary on August 9, 2006.

Instead of telling Kevin he was going to be a big star, Gladys told him to "just be the best he could be." Saying she can't emphasize it enough, Gladys touched on how her approach to motherhood was not about pushing. "I always wanted Kevin's choices and decisions

Galina Cohen

Mother of SASHA COHEN

"Never make an important decision when you are upset."

Galina Cohen is the mother of one of the best figure skaters in the world, Sasha Cohen, who won her first Olympic silver medal at the 2006 Winter Olympics in a performance that many experts said was one of the most remarkable in figure skating history. It's Galina's parenting style of giving Sasha outlets for her abundant energy and guiding but never pushing that Galina said was crucial to helping Sasha achieve all that she has. More than that, Galina said Sasha and her younger sister, Natasha, both describe Galina as "their best friend." After her Olympic success, Sasha was featured on *The Tonight Show with Jay Leno, Jimmy Kimmel Live!, The Ellen DeGeneres Show,* as well as *Live with Regis and Kelly.*

When she's not training for the 2010 Olympics, Sasha supports the Connecticut Children's Medical Center, is a spokesperson for Girls, Inc. and Covenant House, and, through Soldier's Angels, sponsors military personnel who serve in foreign countries.

Galina, who was raised in Russia, said her parents weren't very involved in the daily details when she was growing up. "In Russia, you didn't have your parents as involved because kids pretty much went to their own activities. . . . It's not like living in this country where parents actually have to drive you everywhere." This experience shaped how Galina approaches parenting. "Because of my experience growing up, I want my kids to feel like they're really important to me."

Galina said Sasha was "a really precocious baby." "She did everything early." Still, Galina didn't encourage this, and just let it happen naturally. Letting Sasha develop at her own pace, even if it meant she fell down occasionally, is how Galina has continued to parent. "Sasha was a real risk-taker. The moment she started walking she had nothing but bumps all over her forehead. Every day she got a new bump because she would knock into something. She didn't walk, she ran." Instead of becoming anxious about this, Galina said she enjoyed seeing Sasha's fearlessness.

Galina paid careful attention to what stimulated Sasha as a preschooler. She loved to manipulate things so Galina bought her toys that let her do that. "I would buy her those books where you could push or pull a paper in the book and instead of a word, a little thing would appear that represented that word."

Galina was the strictest when it came to TV. "The TV was never on. As a matter of fact, my kids always reminisce that their friends knew about all these different shows and they had no idea what their friends were talking about." Music, however, filled that entertainment void. "We loved Peter, Paul, and Mary, and we listened to *Beethoven Lives Upstairs*."

Galina described Sasha as someone who always marched to her

own drummer. "Sasha always just did her own thing," a streak of independence that would be critical in achieving her Olympic goals. In fact, she marched to her beat so much that Galina said, "We actually had to have her tested, because the teacher was convinced that she had a hearing problem, because she was very loud and didn't respond to the teacher. So we took her to the doctor, and he said, 'You have a very smart little girl who hears very, very well. She just ignores the stuff she doesn't want to listen to.'" However, as opposed to taking that as a sign that Sasha was obstinate, or a "problem child," Galina took it as an indication that Sasha needed to go to a different school. "There were never, you know, bad notes, like your child misbehaved. It was more, Okay, she did a cartwheel on the lawn. And the next was she wanted to finish drawing her picture when everybody was told to put the picture aside. It was never anything disrespectful to teachers." It was this technique of trying to work *with* Sasha's independent streak, as opposed to against it, that Galina employed with her daughter. "Even when she was young there was no point in trying to have her do what I wanted her to do because she just didn't hear me. . . . I just accepted who she was."

Just because Galina accepted who Sasha was didn't mean she let her daughter run wild. To the contrary, Galina realized the specific areas where Sasha needed to be directed and parented accordingly. For example, seeing that Sasha had a lot of energy, Galina would take her to the playground, but then let her do her own thing. "She was so fast, so she would run back and forth, she had so much energy." Since Sasha had so much vigor and talent, Galina tried to funnel it into as many as activities as possible. "She did ballet. She did gymnastics. She did art classes. She did pottery. We pretty much tried everything." Galina emphasized that she never pushed Sasha into these activities. "I've seen too many mothers get their kids in something and their kids would be screaming and crying, 'I don't want to stay here. Take me out of here, Mom.' I never subscribed to that philosophy. I kind of said, 'Well, if you really don't want to be here, then we're going to get out of here,' which we did."

Galina described Sasha as the one who pushed herself into a more aggressive skating schedule, displaying the kind of self-motivation that any Olympic athlete needs. "She said to me, 'I want to come one extra time a week, just to skate on my own and not just in a lesson.' I would come and drop her off and she would skate and then I would pick her up afterward." Galina stressed that she did not have expectations of Sasha, which, ironically, has helped her exceed everyone else's expectations. "To me sports are just a healthy part of a child's development. That's all it is. I remember the coach told me, 'Well, you know, we should enter Sasha in a competition.' And I remember looking at him, I was totally baffled, and I go, 'Why?'"

Like most elements of the Cohens' life, Galina described her close bond with Sasha as evolving organically. However, it's a connection that was cultivated by a lot of quality family time. "We'd always spend weekends together as a family; we loved cooking together. . . . It's a favorite activity. . . . We'd always be around the kitchen, cooking, preparing meals, baking, making truffles, making chocolate mousse, making soufflé, and having friends over who loved doing the same kinds of activities."

Almost as ironic as Galina not having expectations for her Olympic medalist daughter is the fact that Sasha wasn't very good at ice-skating for a long time. "She didn't move fast in skating. She moved very slowly, actually. So you know a lot of kids by that age were into competitive skating. A lot of kids could already do quite a few jumps by the time she started. And she didn't have the coordination to begin with, and that was really hard for her. It took her a long time to master that coordination. A lot longer than it usually takes kids."

At a crucial moment, Sasha's career could have either been made or broken, and it was Galina who stepped in and encouraged her to persevere. "There was a period of time when she said, 'I don't know. I'm just not getting anywhere. Everybody just got the double axle. It's so easy for them and I can't do it. Maybe I shouldn't be in this sport.' And I remember having a conversation with her then and I said, 'Well, you know, if you want to quit, that's fine. But you should never make an important decision when you are this upset. You know, you should never just kind of make a decision on the spur of the moment. You should give yourself time. . . . You've already put three years in the sport . . . give yourself six to eight weeks, and if you feel the same way at the end, then you quit." The rest is history—thanks to a mother who knew exactly when to push and when to hold back.

Florence Corcoran

Mother of BARBARA CORCORAN

"Be there when they come home from school. Be there when they fall down. Be there when they're fresh to straighten them out."

Florence Corcoran, the mother of Barbara Corcoran—the real-estate mogul who has turned New York's Corcoran Group into a five-billion-dollar business—said she always loved kids, which is good because she had ten of them, falling just three short of the thirteen she wanted! Although it was difficult to be in the spotlight as one of ten, Barbara has certainly made her way there in her career. Besides her real-estate success, Barbara recently ventured into television production and business consulting with her new company, Barbara Corcoran Inc., and in a very public ode to her mother she wrote a national bestseller—*Use What You've Got and Other Business Lessons I Learned from My Mom*. Barbara lives with her husband, Bill, and her two children, Tom and Kate, in New York City.

Florence said that Barbara's birth order—she was the second of ten—didn't influence how much attention she received. "Barbara never wanted attention. She was the queen bee." Growing up surrounded by so many siblings, Florence described a lively, family-oriented household. "We ate dinner together every night. We would spend every weekend together as a family. . . . We'd go to the park by the river and bring a lunch. We went roller-skating. My husband's parents were also very much involved. They lived half a mile away." In addition to these daily family rituals, religion was also part of Barbara's everyday life. "They all went to Catholic school," Florence said.

Seeing signs of Barbara's intense focus at a young age—the focus that would help put her at the helm of a multibillion-dollar company—Florence recalled that she could leave little Barbara somewhere and two hours later you would find her in the same spot. "I remember once I went to New York, and I left her with the neighbor, and she said that Barbara didn't move from that spot." With all those kids, Florence said she didn't have time to get worried, but also just generally wasn't anxious about Barbara hitting certain milestones. "She walked at eighteen months, and didn't stop running from that day on," exuding from an early age the type of energy you'd expect of an entrepreneur who would start a billion-dollar business with $1,000 she borrowed from her boyfriend.

As proof that you don't need to sign your child up for every class imaginable for them to be successful, Florence didn't enroll Barbara in *any* classes. Rather, Florence said the built-in network of siblings and family was Barbara's main source of entertainment and stimulation growing up. "I never really had to encourage my children to be social. They were all very social naturally. In fact, they used to put on music and dance shows with each other right in the house. My husband would play the guitar and they would all sing the song."

Florence said she had high expectations of Barbara but was also hands-off about it, letting Barbara realize her own interests and talents. "The kids did what they felt like doing. . . . They had free range of what their abilities were. . . . If they wanted to draw, I would make sure they had paper. If they wanted a certain song, I'd get a record for them."

Florence saw sparks of Barbara's leadership and creativity from the time she was young. "Barbara always made up games and said, 'You're this and you're that, and you do this and you do that,' and they all looked up to her . . . in her own way, she was already in business." With ten children, Florence said she was "lucky if she had time to talk to Barbara." But this was also critical to Barbara's upbringing, as it cultivated a resourcefulness that helped her become such a self-starter. "I never had to worry about her on a rainy day because she would be entertaining herself."

Although Florence would "let Barbara go with her imagination," she said her parenting style was "very controlling." "There were rules and regulations and they had to be obeyed. . . . They had to be home at five-thirty. Nobody could be late." But it was more than just being places on time; Florence was strict about the children "not doing fresh things to other people." She described her parenting style as showing her love through "doing things" rather than through affection. "I used to say, 'Your father has the time for the affection. I show my love for you through my work,' making their clothes, washing their clothes, etc."

Florence said that because Barbara grew up with dyslexia—a learning disability that makes it difficult to read—she was a "very poor student." Florence added, however, that she wasn't very concerned, an attitude that actually allowed Barbara to overcome her learning disability and become an avid champion for the cause. All the profits from her book go to fund the specialized education of dyslexic children. Still, Florence wasn't completely hands-off when it came to school. "I made sure Barbara did all of her homework, and we always helped her with it. . . . I was also involved with the PTA. I painted all the furniture in the kindergarten and made it look like new."

More than telling Barbara to dream big, Florence said her parenting was defined by trying to make her children "nice and good people more than anything." It was also her approach of "sugar mixed with a big dose of spice" that she said she used with her children. "My children tell me I hollered a lot, but I took care of them very well." Most important, Florence said, "I always had a sense of humor."

Florence said the most salient feature of her parenting style was just being there. "Be there when they come home from school. Be there when they fall down, and be there when they're fresh to straighten them out." Putting her parenting approach in the simplest of terms, she said, "You give a child a good home, you feed them properly, and you treat them like human beings, they have to grow up halfway decent." Or, in Barbara's case, 100 percent "decent."

Yvonne Cowie

Mother of COLIN COWIE

"Set limits because children's determination sometimes gets the best of them."

*G*loria Cowie—the mother of Colin Cowie, the man who has been dubbed "the twenty-first-century arbiter of style"—said that an eye for design is something that is in the gene pool. "I was always into design," Gloria said. "Just like me, Colin always had to have the table set just right." Colin has gone on to create an empire out of "having the table set just right." He is the author of seven books about style, weddings, and entertaining. His company, Colin Cowie Lifestyle, has clients ranging from *Architectural Digest* to Oprah Winfrey to Middle Eastern royalty. Colin appears regularly as a popular lifestyle consultant for the *CBS Early Show* and *The Oprah Winfrey Show*. In addition, Colin has designed and produced some of the most talked about multimillion-dollar parties and celebrations around the world. He is a respected consumer products designer and has designed collections for Lenox, JCPenney, and HSN. Born in Kitwe, Zambia, and educated in South Africa, Colin is still in the South African community, giving his time and support to the Phelophepa Train, a provider of health services in rural communities of South Africa, as well as other local South African charitable organizations.

Yvonne recalled that attention was not an issue when Colin, the youngest of four children, was growing up. "He was the baby in the family. He got all the attention he wanted." Happy to let her son develop at his own pace, Yvonne said that she wasn't anxious, nor did she push him to hit certain developmental milestones. "With four children, you had to be content to let things happen on their own," Yvonne said. However, she didn't have a completely laissez-faire attitude toward parenting—Yvonne kept her kids on a tight schedule growing up and didn't allow much TV watching. "I had to be a disciplinarian as far as the TV was concerned."

When it came to nurturing Colin's enthusiasms, Yvonne explained that her approach was fairly simple. "I really didn't do anything that special. I just encouraged all the things that Colin loved, the things that made him happy. . . . He loved music, so we'd encourage him to pursue it. When he was fifteen, we signed him up for organ lessons. Then, either my husband or I would take him to the lesson." Yvonne said she saw her role as the mere *facilitator* of these interests. "He really excelled on his own."

Today, the roots of Colin's multifaceted career can be traced back to the array of activities that Colin participated in when he was younger. In addition to music, Colin was also a talented actor. Yvonne recalled, "Colin loved doing school plays. He once did *Joseph and the Technicolor Dreamcoat*." Colin's artistic abilities and interests didn't stop at music and theater. Even at fifteen, Colin had an eye for design and a hunger for fashion. Yvonne recalled that his allowance did not cover his clothing habit, so he got a job working on the sales floor of a fashionable store. "That was the only way he could afford his clothing habit." Naturally, though, his job turned into an opportunity for entrepreneurship and innovation. "Colin saw that he could do a better job designing the store windows, so, naturally, he started dressing the windows."

When Colin was thirteen years old, his father died. "When he died, my mother lost her soul mate," Colin said. "I knew I was the one who had to pick up the pieces." For Colin, picking up the pieces meant maintaining the traditions his father started. "Colin's father was always the one who organized Christmas dinner. His dad was the ringleader and Colin felt that the torch was passed on to him to keep up the tradition in the house. Even now, he still comes home every June and July, when Australians celebrate the holiday because of the opposite seasons, to organize the dinner."

Asked how Colin had such a deep sense of responsibility at a young age, Yvonne said it was all about the dinner table. "We'd always all sit around and have supper, and everyone would talk about their days. We were a very close family. We really were." Pinpointing specifically what made them such a stable family unit, Yvonne said, "Love."

But in the Cowie household, love was also about setting boundaries. "Colin was a very determined child. I would even say demanding. I had to set limits with him because his determination sometimes got the best of him." A believer in not letting kids get away with things, Yvonne described her parenting approach as "very firm." "I was adamant that he did certain things, like his homework, and I saw that those things got done." Yvonne's involvement in Colin's school extended beyond just making sure he did his assignments. "We belonged to the PTA, and the school used to have nights for fund-raising and my husband and I got very, very involved."

Yvonne is hesitant to take credit for everything Colin has accomplished. "I think I was influential in the sense that I tried to help Colin do what he wanted to do, but he really did it on his own." Circling back to the idea of love—the glue that held her family together—Yvonne said that her approach to mothering is best captured by the idea that she loved each of her children "for a hundred different reasons." For Yvonne, it's the potent combination of love and encouragement—tempered with some discipline—that was the well-designed blueprint she used to help Colin get where he is today.

Jenny Crawford-Mulof

Mother of CINDY CRAWFORD

"When you are concerned with helping people and being a responsible member of the community, those values develop great people. Sometimes getting too focused on 'Aren't you wonderful!' doesn't necessarily develop strong people."

*J*enny Crawford-Mulof—the mother of Cindy Crawford, the iconic supermodel—said that although Cindy was certainly a beautiful child, she was more interested in finding a cure for cancer than becoming a model. "At nine years old, when her brother, Jeffery, had leukemia, I definitely saw her becoming a doctor." Although Cindy didn't become a doctor, she has certainly made her mark on the world in myriad other ways. Cindy graduated from high school as valedictorian and attended Northwestern University on an academic scholarship to study chemical engineering, before dropping out to pursue a full-time modeling career.

During the 1980s and 1990s, Cindy was among the most popular supermodels, from magazine covers to runways to fashion campaigns. Cindy has been featured on the cover of over six hundred magazines, and in 1995, she was ranked as the most highly paid model in the world by *Forbes* magazine. In addition to modeling, Cindy owns her own production company, Crawdaddy Inc. She produced her successful *Cindy Crawford Shape Your Body* workout video and *The Next Challenge*, hosted MTV's *House of Style*, starred in numerous commercials, authored the book *Cindy Crawford Basic Face*, and was featured in the movie *Fair Game*. Cindy donates both her time, energy, and income to breast and ovarian cancer research as well as to the Leukemia Society of America in memory of her brother, Jeffrey. Cindy and her husband, Rande Gerber, have two children.

Having been raised in a lower-income family, Jenny said, impacted the way she brought up Cindy. "It made me instill in her that you have to save and be careful with money, and to also appreciate what we did have. But I have to say, I wasn't particularly aware of how much money I had growing up." Cindy's being the second of four children, Jenny said, did not impact the amount of attention she received. "I had my kids when I was so young. Cindy was born when I was nineteen, so she was like a doll to me. I played with her so much." Being a younger mother, Jenny said, actually worked to her advantage. "I think because I was a young mother, I probably spent more time playing with both girls than a lot of moms do." Describing a built-in network of activities and friends, Jenny recalled how she used to have tea parties and dress-up parties. "I also started babysitting when Cindy was probably about a year old, so I had six other kids at the house. We had a huge area in the house set up with library books."

Jenny's mother, Cindy's grandmother, played a crucial role in Cindy's upbringing—from education to just being around. "My mother was a huge advocate of reading and actually sold *World Books* [encyclopedias] at the time, so we always had the *World Books* and we utilized them a lot." Proximity also enabled a close relationship with both sets of grandparents. "My parents lived in the same town, and so did Cindy's other grandparents," Jenny said.

For Jenny, her expectations for Cindy were rooted in her own upbringing—and the desire for her to have financial independence. "I didn't go to high school, so I wanted my girls to be able to know that they could take care of themselves and that they wouldn't have to depend on anyone else, so my expectations for Cindy were for her to grow in that direction."

Describing herself as a "strict" parent, Jenny said she expected her children, at a very young age, to get dressed and have their beds made before they came down for breakfast. Jenny recalled, "Many times I'd have to remake a bed after they went to school, but it was just part of giving them responsibility and a sense of being a part of the whole family dynamics. I wanted them to have things they were responsible for." Jenny credited her stricter approach of "no wiggle room" as one of the sources of stability in their lives. "My kids knew where the boundaries were at a fairly young age."

As Cindy got older, the rules stayed equally as strict. "If my kids were playing and somebody did something that was not acceptable for my kids, I would say, 'That doesn't work here at this house.'" In Cindy's teenage years, when driving and cars were thrown into the equation, Jenny said she was vigilant about who she let her daughter drive with. "I told her, 'If you can't pick friends who are responsible . . . I'll have to pick you up.'" Instead of making Cindy rebel, Jenny said, this approach made her become more responsible. "My kids were the ones to say to their friends, 'You have to have me home by this time.'"

When she discussed how living with a brother with a terminal illness affected Cindy, Jenny said, "I didn't have as much time to praise them. I wasn't cold, but my son was ill during a pretty crucial time for Cindy. She was seven when we were going through the worst of it with Jeffrey." Jeffrey's illness had a ripple effect on the whole family, and, as Jenny put it, required Cindy and her sisters to mature faster than other kids. "It was over a two-hour drive to where I took Jeffrey to the doctor. I would go and be gone almost all day and come home tired. The girls were aware that I was under a lot of extra stress and really stepped up to the plate." Even with the immense hardship of losing her son to leukemia, Jenny said that she is so lucky to have the four best kids anybody could have asked for. Others, however, tell her it's more than good fortune. "Everybody always tells me that it wasn't that much luck, Jenny. They say, 'You started your kids out on the right foot.'" Although a lot of what Jenny discussed about her parenting approach was certainly a conscious effort, she also described an element of just following her gut. "I think that forty years ago we, as parents, did many things more unconsciously than we do today. I think people sometimes overthink the situation."

Although Jenny said she wasn't "gushy affectionate," she did have a nighttime routine with the children. "Every night they had a bath and got a little treat." In fact, routines were a large part of the Crawford-Mulof household. "Sunday morning was always church and then usually we had a big Sunday dinner, and because both our families lived here in town, many times we would go to one parent or another and spend the afternoon there. I had sisters who weren't that much older than my kids; my kids loved going to their grandma's house and spending time with their cousins." More than anything, Jenny emphasized these family times as what defined Cindy's childhood. "Family togetherness was just a very important part of our whole meaning. I think we just truly cared about each other. . . . We weren't looking for the million-dollar lifestyle." Outside of the family realm, Jenny said she made a concerted effort to be involved in Cindy's life as well. "I was active in the PTA, I was a Girl Scout leader, a room mother, and a Sunday school teacher. I was very family-focused. . . . My life pretty much came down to being and doing stuff with the kids."

Jenny made a point to openly communicate with Cindy about her life plan and also about the harder things, such as financial limitations. "We would talk about how I probably couldn't afford to send her to the best schools, so if she got good grades in junior high and high school, she could get scholarships. . . . I wanted to help her plan how she could get where she wanted to be." As the industrious businesswoman she is, Cindy got involved in modeling as a way to put herself through college. Jenny supported Cindy's decision to venture into modeling but, like any mother, "feared all the terrible things you always hear about the industry." Crediting Cindy's enormous intelligence, Jenny said, "Being pretty wasn't enough for models, movie stars, or anybody. You better be smart, too, and Cindy certainly was and is."

As she looked back, Jenny saw motherhood as a work in progress. "But I think part of making mistakes is a learning process, and I think sometimes even the kids learn when you make mistakes. . . . I wanted Cindy to know that you could face some negative things and that it wouldn't be the end of the world." It's Jenny's tough-love approach and eye toward the "bigger picture" that she said helped get Cindy where she is today. "When you are concerned with helping people and being a responsible member of the community, those values develop great people. Sometimes getting too focused on 'Aren't you wonderful!' doesn't necessarily develop strong people." As proud as Jenny is of her daughter, she said her approach to parenting was more about standing back and enjoying her daughter's success, not trying to live vicariously through it. "I was able to be there and be happy for Cindy without feeling that's who *I* am. I didn't need, or want, her to be who I am." Today, more than emphasizing her professional success, Jenny said, "Cindy has fulfilled my dreams as far as just being a good person." Delineating the role nurture and nature played in Cindy's life, Jenny said, "I think that genetics played a big part of it, but I definitely think that nurture is the defining thing that plays a part in all our lives."

Sophie Florio

Mother of TOM AND STEVE FLORIO

"If you want respect from your children, you have to respect them. If you want love from your children, you have to love them."

Sophie Florio, the mother of two Condé Nast publishing executives—Tom and Steve Florio—is a testament to the American Dream. At fourteen, Sophie went to work at what she described as the "best beauty salon in Woodhaven," a decision that enabled her sons to have the upbringing that would help catapult them into two of the most high-powered jobs in magazine publishing today. Steve was the president, CEO, and vice chairman of Condé Nast, a company responsible for some of the most venerable periodicals in the business, including *Vanity Fair*, *Vogue*, *The New Yorker*, and *Glamour*. Tom, the younger of the two, is the publishing director of *Vogue*, the iconoclastic women's fashion magazine that influences what millions of women wear and buy around the world.

While her sons have gone on to be the purveyors of high-brow culture, Sophie and her husband came from very modest backgrounds—something that certainly shaped how they both approached parenting. "No matter how tired I was, we always ate together. My father always put the best food on the table. . . . We were low income, but we lived like we were rich." Eating together every night was a ritual that continued through the ups and the downs. Sophie stressed that even if there was tension or turmoil, they would still sit down together. "It was very important for me that we sit together and eat. Sometimes there was a misunderstanding, but so what? So what? We would still eat together."

Sophie said that Tom and Steve both hit developmental milestones very early, not surprising in light of what her sons have achieved. "Tom and Steve were crawling, walking, and talking when they were ten months," she recalled. Reaching these benchmarks "ahead of schedule" was not because Sophie pushed and prodded; in fact, quite the opposite. Sophie described her parenting approach as just giving them love, and sitting back and following her sons' enthusiasms. "You know, their whole life we encouraged them, we comforted them, we loved them to death. We thought they were very smart, and we just let them take their own lead."

The only area where Sophie did push was when it came to education. "You know, I never said, 'You have to do this, you have to do that,' we never did that. The only thing that I insisted on was that they were educated." Speaking exclusively in "we" statements, Sophie said her marriage to her husband—one that spanned over fifty years—was the linchpin of their close family. Still, as is often the case, Sophie said that she and her husband did sometimes disagree about how to parent, but they never let her sons in on it. "We would always present a united front."

As part of her emphasis on education, Sophie said she was

"fussy" about who her kids interacted with. "If I thought they were playing with a child who used bad language, I would discourage Steve and Tom from playing with them." However, this hardly limited Steve and Tom's social network. They were involved in all kinds of activities, demonstrating from a young age the breadth of interests that they would later need to run a company with such an eclectic group of publications. "We had many books about artists. My husband would show them films and even if they had friends over, they would sit there and watch, and that's how they became so familiar with the arts." When it came to the daily things, such as manners, Sophie said she was vigilant about saying "thank you." "My husband would say, 'Why are you constantly thanking them for picking up?' I just thought that's how you raise well-mannered children, by modeling good manners yourself."

Upon reflection, Sophie said that Steve and Tom landing at the top of their fields hardly came out of the blue. "As children, they were just so sharp in their thinking, in their decisions, and the way they chose their friends." Sophie said that it wasn't her encouragement to go into publishing that got Steve and Tom where they are today. Rather, she attributed it to letting them have the opportunity to explore the things that interested them, and always letting them know that she was there to bounce ideas off of. "If they got to a point where they were discouraged . . . I was there for them."

Sophie also said she parented by example. "In my own life, I had the drive and I worked hard." Explaining how this work ethic influenced her sons, Sophie said, "I carried that mentality of always working hard right into my own family." Leading by example, just like his mother, Steve became a role model to his younger brother, Tom. "I think Tom looked up to his brother. He had the drive. He tried finance first, but he wasn't happy. Then he worked for a magazine after graduation, and he liked it. Then there was a position open at *Vanity Fair,* and he just flew." Modeling a strong example for her sons is still something she prides herself on today. "I went back to college at age fifty-something and became a high school teacher and got a full-time position at the high school."

Sophie said that although religion was not a daily part of Steve and Tom's life, they went to church often. "They were baptized, had communion, and confirmation. . . . We all prayed. . . . Before we had our meals we would hold hands and ask the Lord to bless the food . . . and I see today that Steve and Tom are bringing their kids up that same way."

For Sophie, encouraging her sons was just about the effective use of simple phrases like: "You're great. You're smart. You're wonderful. I'm so proud of you. I knew you could do it. I always had faith in you." Sophie credited this approach to the reciprocal relationship she has with her sons today. "They think I'm the most wonderful, beautiful, magnificent mother . . . I absolutely adored them and they knew it. They know it now."

When asked how she imparted a value as abstract as respect, Sophie said she accomplished it through always listening to her sons. "I listened and listened, and they knew if they wanted to discuss any little thing, they could." Distilling her parenting approach down to its essence, Sophie said it was, and is, about the giving out of what you want to get back. "If you want respect from your children, you have to respect them. If you want love from your children, you have to love them. . . . I also didn't tolerate any nonsense, but I was very fair."

Diane Fine

Mother of STEFANI GREENFIELD

"I would tell her that she was great, but I would also tell her when she wasn't so good."

*D*iane Fine, the mother of Stefani Greenfield—cofounder of the wildly successful Scoop boutique franchise—said that Stefani was always a trendsetter, even when she was growing up. "She wore what she wanted to wear, even in those days when kids were very peer conscious. If everybody was wearing a brown jacket and she wanted to wear a yellow jacket, she would wear a yellow jacket and couldn't care less." It was this fiercely independent streak, coupled with her eye for fashion, that led Stefani to start one of the most successful clothing store chains in the country. Working her way up from Donna Karan to Esprit, Stefani first conceptualized "The Ultimate Closet," which later became known as Scoop. In addition to running a fleet of stores, Stefani is actively involved with many charities and is a cofounder of Love Heals, the Alison

Gertz Foundation for AIDS Education. Regarded as a national authority on style, Stefani is a regular fashion contributor to the *Today* show and created and hosts a show on HSN called *Scoop Style*. Stefani and her husband, Mitchell, welcomed their first daughter, Theodora Suki Silverman, in January 2007.

Diane said that, from the time Stefani was an infant, she displayed signs of the powerhouse she would go on to become. "Stefani started to crawl at nine months, she walked at a year . . . by the time she was eight months old, she was saying many words, and by nineteen months she spoke in full sentences . . . she hasn't stopped since." Parenting such an overachiever allayed any of Diane's anxiety about Stefani reaching certain developmental benchmarks, because, as she put it, "Stefani was way above whatever milestones were established."

Although Stefani seemed to hit all these milestones way ahead of schedule, Diane said she was still vigilant about reading to Stefani. "I read to her, and her father read to her. It was part of the daily routine." Along with highly developed verbal skills, Stefani was also ahead of the curve when it came to doing things on her own. "She was born independent," Diane said. Without the plethora of "Mommy and Me" classes that parents have available to them today, Diane said it was their network of friends that was the main source of Stefani's social and intellectual stimulation. "We lived in an apartment building and it was very easy to be social. Everybody that lived there had little children."

Honing Stefani's strengths and trying to augment her weaknesses was the approach that Diane took with her daughter. "Stefani wasn't very athletic, but she was very creative and she had a fantastic memory. I mean, Stefani was reading fluently in kindergarten." Still, Diane didn't focus on the fact that Stefani was such an overachiever and instead opted for a more laid-back approach. "I really wanted her to do whatever she wanted. I felt like she could do a lot of things, but I didn't make a big deal about it." More than anything,

Diane said she chose activities to advance Stefani's already advanced verbal skills. "When she decided that she recognized words, I had a million stickers all over the house . . . everything had a sticker on it."

Diane's essential recipe for parenting was equal parts discipline and understanding. "I was strict about putting your room together. You had to do your homework; you had to go to sleep on time. You know, those kinds of things." As part of her balanced parenting style, Diane said that she would give Stefani feedback about the good *and* the bad. "I would tell her that she was great, but I would also tell her when she wasn't so good."

Even though Diane and her husband divorced, Diane made a concerted effort to keep a sense of normalcy in Stefani's life. "We would eat together almost every night of the week." Religion was also an important part of keeping the family intact. "The kids went to Hebrew school, and we observed the holidays." Diane was involved at her children's school. "I was always active in their school life, the PTA, meetings with teachers." Diane named "just being there" as one of the things she prioritized above all else. "I felt like it was important to be home when they came home from school. I had to take them places. I wanted to know what they were doing, so I was usually home by three or four."

Diane attributed Stefani's enormous success today to her independence and to weathering hardships in life. "Even though divorce can be very negative, I think for Stefani it might have been what pushed her to be what she is today. . . . She always had to do certain things for herself, or figure things out, or overcome being hurt and she managed to do that by herself. She's a very strong, independent person."

Overcoming obstacles and learning to be self-reliant, while crucial to Stefani's success, are only part of it. Diane said that above all else Stefani was, and is, a hard worker, a quality modeled for her by a mother who always worked. "When Stefani was a senior at

Stuyvesant High School, her father and I told her that she could not hang around, and that she had to get a job. We thought, however, 'Who is going to give her a job on Saturday and Sunday?' When she came home that day, she had landed a job at a store on Madison Avenue called American High. At first, they told her that they didn't hire students. So she said to them, 'Why don't you let me come tomorrow, and I'll work for you for nothing. You'll see. I'm going to be terrific, and you'll hire me.' Stefani did that for two days, and they hired her."

It was this quality of tenacity and "not taking things lying down" that Stefani picked up through osmosis and careful observation of a mother who did the same in her own life. Reflecting, Diane said, "I developed a whole career after I was divorced; I went back to school and worked. Stefani saw all of that." But like any successful entrepreneur, Stefani did more than just sit back passively and watch. Instead, she put all those qualities into action in her own life. Diane summed up her approach to parenting as figuring out the yin and yang of your child. "I think you just have to understand what your child's strengths and weaknesses are and focus on the strengths and help them overcome some weaknesses. That's the best you can do."

Nancy Hawk

Mother of TONY HAWK

"We never expected him to become a big star or anything like that. We just figured that skateboarding was really good for him because he loved it."

*N*ancy Hawk, the mother of Tony Hawk—the single most influential skateboarder in the history of the sport—said her advice to parents is to let children have some freedom to explore and find out what they are good at. "Then encourage them unless it's something that's dangerous to them, or something that's not good." While skateboarding might not be the safest sport, this was the credo that Nancy used throughout Tony's life, playing a large part in his litany of accomplishments that extend well beyond skateboarding.

Tony has been a professional skateboarder since the age of fifteen, has won over ninety competitions, and is considered to have the best professional skateboard record in history. He has succeeded in everything from television to movies to music to writing. In 2000, Tony wrote a bestselling autobiography, *HAWK: Occupation: Skateboarder*. He has also made an effort to give back to the sport by founding the Tony Hawk Foundation, an organization that focuses on promoting and financing public skateboard parks in low-income communities throughout the United States. Tony has three children.

Nancy's other parenting mantra was, and is, "I don't stress easily." Even when she was five months pregnant with Tony—at forty-three—and her husband suffered a heart attack, she said she rolled with the punches, manifesting the resilient and dogged attitude that she imparted to her son. In fact, Nancy described Tony as an extremely determined child. "He just had a really good little mind and he grasped things. He was so determined to do everything his way." Intuiting that he needed to figure things out on his own, Nancy said that she didn't push Tony and let him develop at his own pace.

Nancy said that her husband, an active parent like Nancy, coached Tony's basketball league for a while, but Tony soon realized that he didn't like the team dynamic. "He felt that if he wasn't good at something, he was letting the team down if he wasn't perfect. . . . My husband went ahead and kept the team, but Tony just wasn't a part of it. Then, once he learned how to skate, that was all he really wanted to do." Nancy said she encouraged Tony when it came to skateboarding because it was evident that this was his raison d'être. Reflecting on her son's early years of skateboarding, Nancy said, "I don't think that anyone has ever worked harder at their sport than Tony worked at skateboarding."

Nancy's general parenting style was to use more sugar than spice and was not very "disciplinarian," but she was hardly a pushover. "I think that, generally speaking, the kids always knew what the limits were. . . . There were standards. . . . You come home, do your homework, you treat people kindly, you don't lie, you don't cheat."

Nancy said she made a point to encourage Tony, who as a kid was always hard on himself. "I'd always say to him, 'Gee, Tony, I was amazed at how you learned that trick.' Or I'd comment on the amount of time and effort he'd put in." It was this approach, more than constant yelling and hounding from the sidelines, that Nancy said she employed with a son who would go on to set records in his sport. "We never expected him to become a big star or anything like that. We just figured that skateboarding was really good for him because he loved it."

Although skateboarding was a huge part of Tony's life, family played an equally important, if not more central, role in his childhood. Nancy, who was raised by parents who were married for fifty years, said the Hawks would eat dinner together every night. "We would also do lots of family activities together. We were very big on the beaches; whenever the sun was out we would go." In addition to family activities, Nancy and her husband made it clear to the kids that "they came first." Taking that concept to the next level, Tony's father started the National Skateboarding Association when Tony was twelve so he could have the same advantages that baseball and basketball teams had.

Nancy said that as Tony advanced in his skateboarding career he had less time for academics, but still was able to maintain a solid "B" average. When it came to being involved in school, Nancy, like many parents today who juggle so much, said that as a working mom she didn't always have time. "I had been the PTA president when my other children were in school, but when I was working there just wasn't time."

Making Tony a well-rounded person was a priority for Nancy, so she exposed Tony to a wide variety of cultures and places, contributing to the breadth and depth of his interests and accomplishments today. "One of the things I said to him was that I wanted him to go and look at art books, so we did that. He always had an interest in art."

When it came time for Tony to decide between his skateboarding career and college, Nancy let Tony make up his own mind. "We sort of always assumed that when the skateboarding was over he would go on to college and have a career, but then skateboarding got so big and he was doing so well. We never encouraged him to stop and go to college because I started college late in life, and I figured anybody can go to college whenever they want to."

Even with all the parental involvement and encouragement that Tony had growing up, Nancy attributed Tony's incredible accomplishments to his own drive. "I think that his success is really based on him. He has a bright mind." However, it was a drive cultivated by a mother who let him have enough room to test the limits of how far his own motivation would take him. "When Tony was seventeen, a company sold his board and they paid Tony a dollar a board, and they would sell twenty thousand a month. . . . That's a lot of money for a kid to have. But when someone asked us, 'What do you do with Tony's money?' I said, 'It was always Tony's money. It always went in the bank for him.' Then he bought his first house the day before he was eighteen." Asked how she did it, Nancy said, "My priority has just always been my children."

Mary Higgins Clark

Mother of CAROL HIGGINS CLARK

"Just do well and be your own person."

ary Higgins Clark—the bestselling author whose books have sold over eighty-five million copies in the United States alone, and mother of author Carol Higgins Clark—said that all of her five children are storytellers. "At the dinner table, Carol, who is the fourth of my five, learned very quickly that if you told a boring story, you would get cut off immediately. The rough-and-tumble of growing up with four siblings made Carol, and all of them for that matter, enhance their natural wit." Today Carol is a bestselling author of ten novels who also has collaborated on four Christmas novels with her mother.

Reflecting on how she has been blessed in both the big and little things in life, Mary said that with Carol, "I never had to nag her to do her homework. She always had it started by the time I got home." Asked about how she scheduled Carol's time as a child, Mary said, "It was just a different world then. You didn't have playdates. All the kids lived on the same block and they just got together spontaneously."

Following in her mother's writing footsteps was not the path that Carol initially intended. After graduating from Mount Holyoke College, she studied acting—a discipline that is definitely related to writing, according to Mary. "When you are acting, you are a character in a story, and being able to make that character compelling and believable is what makes you a good actor. As an actor and a writer you have to understand what makes humor work and why it may or may not work."

For Carol, becoming an author was not a result of her mother's encouragement, but rather the consequence of a fortuitous sequence of events. Mary explained, "When Carol was eighteen, I had to re-type a whole manuscript and August was the busiest month of the year, since I was producing forty radio programs, and I just couldn't find a minute to type. Carol was home from college, so she did it. As she was retyping she was telling me, 'I don't think that character would say this or that character would say that.' That was when I realized that she had a real talent as a writer. Years later a friend introduced her to Warner Books. She told them her idea for a continuing series with a thirty-year-old private investigator, Regan Reilly, the main character. *Publishers Weekly* gave it a rave review." Today, Carol's Regan Reilly mysteries are hugely popular and she continues to cowrite with Mary Higgins Clark. In addition, Carol has appeared in television, film, and theater productions, including the television movie *A Cry in the Night,* based on her mother's novel.

Reflecting further on how she expressed her expectations to Carol, Mary said that a high premium was always placed on doing well and being ambitious. "But I didn't just want them to do well at anything," Mary explained. "I wanted them to explore their natural talents. For example, I never expected anyone to sing in the choir, because we just can't carry a tune in our family."

Mary described her parenting style as one defined by empowering her children to know that she trusted them to make good decisions. "When they were first driving, and I was working a full-time job, I said to them, 'I have to trust you to come home on time because I can't stay up and wait for you.'" It was always a dialogue, even when it came to enforcing rules. "We talked about a reasonable time for them as a curfew. I discussed curfew times with their friends' parents, and we had a solid front."

A believer in praise and encouragement as the centerpieces of how to be a good parent, Mary said, "I always tell parents that when a child shows you a drawing or poem he or she has created, focus on the creativity and forget about the misspelling or that the crayons went outside the lines. Encouragement really does wonders for a child's self-esteem."

Success and hardship have come in equal doses in both Mary's and Carol's lives. When Carol was eight years old, her father, Warren, died. Mary was a young widow with five children ranging in age from five to thirteen. Asked how she weathered this, Mary said, "I felt it was my job to make the children's life as happy as I possibly could; the surviving parent, no matter how grief stricken, cannot fall apart."

The core of Mary's advice to parents is to help your children find the gift that gives them joy. Everyone is good at something. "If they have a good voice, encourage them to be in the choir. I tried giving my children piano lessons, but they were not interested. Ultimately natural talent and interest shows itself." As for the more concrete, Mary said, "Give them a good education. Every parent wants their child to be happy, love what they do, and have a fulfilling emotional and social life. Having a good education will be the cornerstone on which they can build all those things."

Describing their mother-daughter collaborations, Mary aptly used a parent-child metaphor: "When Carol and I write a book together, it's such a collaborative effort. We want the book to be the perfect child. We sometimes come out with a phrase, and the other one will say, 'I was just thinking that.' Our minds are so in sync. It's one voice."

Dot Jeter

Mother of DEREK JETER

"You better practice hard, because there's always someone out there better than you. . . . Don't let anybody outwork you."

Dot Jeter—the mother of Derek Jeter, the eight-time All-Star shortstop and captain for the New York Yankees—said that when Derek was five years old he made it very clear that he was going to play for the Yankees. "In fact, in his eighth-grade yearbook, where it predicted where everyone was going to be in twenty years, it said that Derek was going be the shortstop for the New York Yankees." In June 2004, Derek was named the eleventh captain in Yankee history. He has received the All-Star and World Series MVP Awards and three Gold Glove Awards. Derek has the sixth-highest lifetime batting average for active ballplayers and was the starting shortstop for the USA team in the first-ever World Baseball Classic.

Derek is the president and founder of the Turn 2 Foundation, a charitable organization founded in 1996 to support and encourage youth to "turn to" healthy lifestyles, academic achievement, and leadership development and to avoid drug and alcohol addiction. The foundation provides youth programs in New York, western Michigan, and the Tampa, Florida, area. Derek also heads the Jeter's Leaders Program, a leadership development program for high school students created to empower, recognize, and enhance the skills of students who promote healthy lifestyles, excel academically, are committed to improving their communities and serving as role models to younger students, and deliver positive messages to their peers.

In his baseball career, Derek was named "Most Marketable Player in Baseball" in 2005 and 2006 by *Sports Business Journal* and one of the "Top 100 Celebrities" on *Forbes*'s 2005 list. He has been featured in national advertising campaigns for Nike, Gatorade, Ford Motors, and Avon, among others, and was twice named to *People* magazine's "50 Most Beautiful People" list. Derek hosted *Saturday Night Live* in 2001 and has also appeared on *60 Minutes*, *Seinfeld*, *The Late Show with David Letterman*, and *ESPN Sports-Century*.

Dot said her position as the second of fourteen children in a lower-income family colored how she raised Derek and his sister. "I think the way you are brought up affects the way you bring up your children. There's no doubt about it. For me, it was about teaching Derek the value of working hard, because things certainly weren't handed to me." As part of her parenting philosophy of having to work hard for things, Dot was fairly strict. "There wasn't a lot of TV. I always told them they should be outside playing or doing things. I wanted them to be creative and active." Derek, luckily, had built-in playmates. "During the first four years of his life, I was going to college, so my mom watched him. A lot of my younger siblings were still around, and Derek was able to play with them."

Baseball, however, was not the first sport that Dot tried to get

Derek to participate in. "It's funny because we enrolled him in football at first, and he didn't like that, so we didn't force him to play. Then, when he was four, we enrolled him in baseball, and he stuck with that from then on. . . . Baseball was his whole life." To help Derek channel his determination, Dot and her husband sat down with him and actually wrote out his goals. "When Derek switched from Catholic school to public school, I got a little nervous about him going to such a large school. I wanted him to have some real focus. We made a contract, complete with goals and expectations, and he had to adhere to them, or there were consequences." She adamantly enforced the contract that she had Derek sign. "He knew he would be grounded if he didn't follow the rules. . . . The contract was more than just about grades; it was about respecting people, our home, and using his lunch money for the right things." Dot said that contract worked very well, but Derek, like all children do, had his slips, and Dot saw to it that there were consequences. "If he didn't bring a 4.0, he couldn't play baseball or other sports." Dot recalled, "Once he was grounded for thirty days, and he wasn't allowed to use the car. He had to walk to school, which was really hard on him." She pushed Derek in school because she saw his enormous potential, not because she had some preconceived notion for how a child "should" perform. "I pushed him to get good grades in school because I knew he had it in him."

Dot's style, however, was not to dwell on the negative. "When Derek would do something good, whether it was in school or with a neighbor, we would just say, 'That's really great.'" The paradigm in the Jeter household was not just about punishing the bad, but also about rewarding the good. "If Derek met a certain goal, we would go out to dinner, which was a big deal because we didn't have that much money. We always wanted him to know that we were proud of him." While Derek made it clear from the time he was young that he was going to play for the Yankees, it was a hard goal for Dot to wrap her mind around. "I remember one of his teachers said to me and Derek's father, 'You guys better talk to your son because all he wants to do is play baseball and he thinks he's going to play for the New York Yankees.' And both my husband and I looked at each other and said, 'Why are we going to destroy his dreams?'" Although it seemed like a long shot, Dot kept encouraging Derek, but made sure he knew that it was going to take an intense commitment. "I told him, 'You better practice hard, because there's always someone out there better than you. . . . Don't let anybody outwork you.'" She said that it was a challenge, particularly coming from a small town in Michigan, to imagine Derek going to play for a team like the Yankees. "I said to him, 'I don't want to burst your bubble, but you are going to have to work really, really hard.' He then went on to became the high school player of the year."

In addition to giving words of encouragement, Dot modeled the work ethic she instilled in Derek in her own life. "I always wanted to get that better job. . . . I had the goal of getting a job at this big pharmaceutical company and I didn't know anybody, and I just worked at it and just kept sending my résumé and making phone calls." When it came to her more day-to-day involvement, Dot gave new meaning to "involved parent." "I was on the PTA. I was on the booster club. I was on the fix-up-the-field club. We started a mentor club. . . . I knew all of Derek's friends." The weekends, Dot said, were reserved for family time. "We did everything together, so the weekends were just a natural extension."

Dot's advice to mothers is simple: "Listen to them. Get them things that you know are going to encourage their dreams." Even if they don't have all the "right" physical requirements to play their chosen sport, Dot believes that encouragement can surmount just about anything. "One thing I really don't like is when people say, 'Your child isn't tall enough to play basketball, or he's not smart enough to go to the University of Michigan.' You just have to

Terri Augello

Mother of ALICIA KEYS

"It's a fickle world out there. They could love you today. They can hate you tomorrow. So . . . make sure that you keep your family and friends close around you."

*T*erri Augello, the mother of Alicia Keys—a singer, song-writer, composer, and actor who has sold over forty million albums—said that when Alicia was looking to buy a house a few years back, she asked her Nana if she would consider living with her, which is no small testament to the way Alicia was raised by her mother. Today, Alicia has nine Grammy Awards under her belt. She's performed at a number of charitable events, including the televised benefit concert following September 11; at the worldwide Live Aid concerts; and at events to raise funds for Hurricane Katrina victims.

Alicia is also a spokesperson for Keep a Child Alive (see www.keep-achildalive.org for info) and Frum tha Ground Up (www.ftgu.org) and Teens in Motion (www.teens-in-motion.org), two organizations devoted to inspiring, encouraging, and motivating American youth. She is the author of the bestseller *Tears for Water*. Her third studio album, *As I Am* released in November 2007, has remained on the top of the charts and she's near reaching triple platinum status. Her acting credits began as Maria, a friend of Rudy Huxtable, in *The Cosby Show* when she was five years old. She continues that part of her creative passion in the film *Smokin Aces*, with Jeremy Piven, Ray Liotta, and Ben Affleck, and costarring with Scarlett Johansson in *The Nanny Diaries*, with Paul Giamatti and Laura Linney, both released in 2007, and is presently filming *The Secret Life of Bees* due out at the end of 2008.

It's hardly a surprise that the mother of a nine-time Grammy award–winner said that hard work was always a part of her own life. "When my dad, Alicia's grandfather, passed away when I was twelve, leaving my mom, Donna, a widow with nine children, we were all expected to get a job as soon as we could. We babysat, and we got our working papers as soon as we were old enough." Asked how her upbringing in a lower-middle-class home impacted the way she raised Alicia, Terri said, "It affected it because it made me very aware of the value of having a strong work ethic." She worked through her pregnancy and, as a single mother, was the only source of income for her family. Like so many single mothers, Terri recalled the heart-wrenching experience of leaving her daughter to return to work. "I felt like I was the worst mother in the world. So the first couple of months going back to work felt like such a terrible thing. But the babysitter told me very nicely, as soon as the elevator door closed, that Alicia stopped crying and was just fine."

Terri said that Alicia hit the developmental benchmarks ahead of schedule, as might be expected from someone who released a platinum album at twenty. "She took her first steps before her first birthday," Terri recalled. To encourage Alicia to develop her pool of talents, Terri made sure that reading was a focal point of her daughter's upbringing. "I was so anxious to have books and encyclopedias and loads of reading material, I had a library gathered for her before she was even born. It was a little obsessive, I'll admit." Terri stressed that reading was a collaborative activity for the two of them. "We always read before bedtime and on the weekends. . . . I'd read one paragraph, and she'd read the other. It always was, and still is, a big part of our lives." Terri also made prayer into a bonding experience. "We were spiritual together. . . . We said our prayers before meals and before bedtime."

With such an emphasis on stimulating and expanding Alicia's mind, Terri definitely limited the types of television shows Alicia was allowed to watch. "I remember I was appalled by *Married with Children*. I thought it was pretty disrespectful to women, especially for youngsters unable to grasp the adult sarcasm, and when she got into watching music videos, I really had a lot to say about those. I couldn't stand that kind of misogynistic energy and booty talk in my house."

Terri's somewhat strict approach, at least by today's standards, toward music videos didn't limit Alicia's exposure to music. Terri said there was always music playing in the house when Alicia was growing up. From the time she was in a stroller, Alicia sang songs with Terri, like "Take Me Out to the Ball Game." To encourage her, Terri made up music to all the nursery rhymes. "I often sang her to sleep when she was little." Emphasizing her own love of music, Terri described herself as "a big jazz freak." "I also just love show tunes."

Terri's encouragement of Alicia didn't stop with music and reading. Confessing that she "probably drove Alicia crazy," Terri said that she always had Alicia doing some kind of activity. "I took her to gymnastics, she played neighborhood basketball, she took dance at Alvin Ailey, and began piano lessons at age seven . . . it was always our schedule to get from A to B to C to D." But more important than all these lessons was the fact that when Alicia said to Terri, " 'Mommy, I can't do all of this,' I told her 'that's okay, you can stop dance and gymnastics,' but she had to stick to piano, which was always the stand-out activity for Alicia. When it came to piano, that was something she asked to do." Understanding how important the piano was to her daughter and seeing how talented Alicia was at it, Terri said, "I did whatever I could to make it happen. Whenever she was really just stressed, I'd give her the summer off and then she'd be anxious to go back."

Terri explained that "lessons" were only one component of Alicia's education. "I would also try to impart the value of respect to her through phrases like 'Be respectful of others, and they'll be respectful of you, because you don't know what shoes they're walking in.' " Emphasis was also placed on cultivating Alicia's ability to interact with adults. "When Alicia was little, we lived in an acting community, a performing arts building called 'Manhattan Plaza,' so we always had a lot of friends who would come by. And because I was a single parent, there was a lot of help and support from the community. There was a lot of socialization between the age groups."

Although it might be hard to believe today, in light of what Alicia has accomplished, Terri had no visions of her daughter being a world-renowned performer. Rather, Terri said, it was about giving Alicia the opportunities to find out what *her* passions were. "I had no expectations of her being a 'superstar,' or that she would have enough money to take care of me. I really just went day to day."

Reflecting on her parenting approach, Terri said that it was equal parts nurturing, discipline, and understanding. Respect, however, was the cardinal value. "I wanted her to respect her elders, and I wanted her to respect me and herself." Terri continued by saying that she used respect as a means to open up a dialogue about religion. "I instilled respect in her by teaching her that God was in nature and is in each person . . . so you have to have respect for other people." Possessing this sense of spirituality has helped keep Terri and Alicia grounded. "You know, it's a very fickle world out there. They could love you today. They can hate you tomorrow. So . . . make sure that you keep your family and close friends around you."

Like most teenage daughters, Terri said that Alicia did have her sassy phases. "I would say to her, 'Don't talk to me like you talk to your girlfriends.' By the same token, if I saw someone disrespecting her, we would talk about it." Terri instilled in Alicia the understanding that there was a right way and a wrong way to treat people. "You can't just open your mouth and say whatever you want." As another offshoot of this parenting approach, Terri always told Alicia to be happy for others' achievements, even if they shined more than she did. It was part of Terri's philosophy that talent is not enough—you have to couple it with humility.

Even though Alicia has gone on to become one of the most successful musicians in the industry, her childhood was hardly smooth sailing. Looking back, Terri recognized that she struggled being a single parent. Still, she was vigilant about keeping her problems with Alicia's father separate from her relationship with her daughter. "I felt that my issues with Alicia's father were our problems, not hers. . . . So I left a huge door open for them to establish their relationship as they saw fit." The silver lining, Terri said, was that his parents were the "best grandparents." "We kind of fell into this amazing, loving relationship with them."

For Terri, motherhood and instilling the principles of success were about the big *and* the little things. "I always made her a nice lunch. She recently told me that her friends at school always wanted her lunches!" Motherhood was also about being there in Alicia's teen years. "A lot of parents think that once a child gets to high school, 'I'm finished,' and that's really not true." Terri said Alicia's adolescence was trying, but manageable, because the lines of communication were always kept open. "There was a moment between the age of thirteen and fifteen where she told me she just didn't want to do anything. And she just wasn't happy with the world. I don't know what heaviness had come over her, with puberty and everything else. You never know. So she said, 'Please, Mom, don't bother me. I barely want to go to school.' We worked it out, we talked, and she got herself together, and ended up graduating at age sixteen as valedictorian of her high school senior class." Terri credited her understanding approach, particularly in Alicia's teenage years, to putting herself in her daughter's shoes. "She asked me to just please understand her, and I did my best. . . . I always remembered, too, that I had been a teenager myself and had gone through some of the same struggles."

Still, Terri also prided herself on a no-nonsense approach. "When boys would come to the house, they would have to come meet me. I had to see what they looked like because I wanted to be able to give a description to the police if she didn't come home. . . . Also, if boys called and said something like, 'Yo,' I would say, 'Excuse me, who are you calling? Do you know that you're speaking to a grown-up here?'" Although she was strict, Terri was anything but alienated from Alicia's social circle because of it. "Her friends were always at my apartment."

Terri delineated what has made Alicia so successful, by saying it was a combination of a natural evolution and her strategic guidance. "You know, when you open your child's world to all those books, learning, and film, they learn about dreaming big. Plus, they have to know that their self-worth isn't tied up in what other people think of you." As for Terri's advice to mothers today: "Keep the lines of communication open from the time they can talk, believe and trust in your child's intuitions, and always make opportunities available."

Helen Kirsch

Mother of DAVID KIRSCH

> "Be true to yourself. Money comes and goes, but your
> integrity is something that you have always."

*H*elen Kirsch—mother of fitness guru David Kirsch—is quick to put out the disclaimer that she isn't an expert on parenting. "It doesn't come with any rules. It's the only job in the world that you don't need any training for." With that said, her mark is quite evident in what is now a multimedia David Kirsch empire. David advocates for mind/body conditioning and has used his technique with celebrities like Heidi Klum, Liv Tyler, and Naomi Campbell. David has written many well-received books, such as *Sound Mind, Sound Body.* He has also released a series of videos, including *David Kirsch's One-on-One Training Series*. As founder of Manhattan's Madison Square Club, David combined fitness with his ventures into the nutrition and skin care industries as well as creating a line of nutritional supplements. David is a featured expert on ABC's *Extreme Makeover* and has appeared on *Today, Access Hollywood,* and *Extra* as well as in *Time, Vogue,* the *New York Times,* and *People.* In October 2002, David became a spokesperson for the Almond Board of America and was a panelist, along with Christy Turlington and Dr. Andrew Weil, at the prestigious Bath and Body Works Wellness Summit. David published his third book, *The Ultimate New York Diet,* in November 2006.

From the time he was young, Helen said that she instilled in David the philosophy that life is about the bigger things. "I always told him to be true to yourself and that money comes and goes, but your integrity is something that you have always." Although Helen didn't raise David to be very religious, there was always an element of tradition in the Kirsch household. "My children knew who they were religiously and we went to temple and observed our holidays."

For some mothers, the epiphany that their child is special comes from seeing them in their element later in life, but Helen said she knew from the minute he was born that David was exceptional. "I knew when I picked him up and held him that he was special. He's intuitive. He is honest. His integrity is beyond reproach."

Describing almost a psychic bond with her son, Helen said she has always been connected to him in an almost otherworldly way. "I remember once I fell and I was bleeding and crying and sitting on the floor. I was alone in the house. David was at college and my husband was at work. Five minutes later, the doorbell rang and it was David. He said to me, 'I just knew that you needed me.'" Their bond has thrived over the years. "I speak to David every day. . . . I also help him manage a business venture he just started."

When it came to the more mundane, worldly things, David's childhood was regimented. "He came home, did his homework, took care of chores, and then he was able to relax and watch TV." More than anything, Helen said her parenting style was informed by her deep desire for her children to have lives that they would be the very best at and for them to be happy. "I didn't choose their life for them." Even though her husband of half a century, Herb, was in the health-care field, Helen said they didn't encourage David to follow in his father's footsteps. "We never pushed David. We always just believed if you love it, that's fine, but never do what someone else wants you to do." Today David credits her for his tenacity. "When the days got hard, David said to me, 'You made me think I could do anything.' I'd say to him, 'Dust yourself off and start again.'"

Helen said she has been proud of David all along; the fame was just an added bonus. "David was always a source of pride to us and when people ask me today, 'Aren't you proud of him?' I say, 'I was always proud of David.'" It's why today, more than emphasizing his litany of professional accomplishments, Helen focuses on other things. "David is a very caring, warm person. He's easy to talk to and he's not easily impressed. He knows who he is."

Describing her parenting style as a fusion of strictness and understanding, Helen said she was also a very affectionate mother. Married to Herb for over fifty years, Helen called him her "best friend" and said their marriage was the foundation of their tight-knit family. "A house is built on a foundation and Herb and I were the foundation and the children are the walls." Growing up, the Kirsches enjoyed a myriad of activities together. "We'd go to the beach. We'd play volleyball. We'd have picnics." They were also fortunate enough to have extended family nearby. "I was very close with my siblings. My brother and my sister lived within a radius of about three miles of us. [The children] always saw their aunts and uncles and their cousins. That was very important to me because I never had that." As much emphasis as there was on family time, Helen also wanted her son to be independent. "David started school at four and a half, because I thought it was important for him to be away from me."

Encouragement was something that came easily to Helen. In

fact, Helen said, "I can still hear my friends telling me, 'Do you think David is going to be a movie star?' " Still, for Helen, parenting was an intricate dance. "I think you have to love them enough to let go, because anything you let go of is going to come back." Expanding on that, she said, "You have to think a child, it's a gift. It's a gift that you have sometimes eighteen years, twenty years." When asked the role she played in helping him achieve his successes, Helen credits David for where he is today. "David did it. David did it." And while it's true that "David did it," Helen's "tough love," as she described it, seems to have played a part. "I'm not easy. I expected a lot from David, and I also always try to make the best of everything." Hitting on the truism that "good friends are hard to find," Helen said, "Friends are difficult to leave and impossible to forget. Above all, I consider David my friend."

Tina Knowles

Mother of BEYONCÉ KNOWLES

"We always told her that she could be the best at
what she does, but she has to love it first."

W e absolutely listened to music. Both my husband and I
were in singing groups and we loved all types of music,"
said Tina Knowles, the mother of Beyoncé Knowles, a
founding member of Destiny's Child, one of the bestselling female
groups of all time. Today, there is no doubt that her mother's love
and passion for music has trickled down to Beyoncé. She has earned
a rock-star status that is practically unprecedented for a
twenty-six-year-old. Destiny's Child has sold more than forty million albums and singles worldwide and earned an astounding
twenty-three gold, platinum, and multiplatinum certifications. As
an individual performer, Beyoncé has earned Grammy Awards,
American Music Awards, World Music Awards, and the prestigious

NAACP Image Award. In 2001, Beyoncé become the first African-American woman to win the ASCAP Pop Songwriter of the Year Award.

Beyoncé toured America for the first time as a solo artist in 2004 to promote her multiplatinum debut solo album, *Dangerously in Love*, which earned her five Grammy Awards, including Best Contemporary R&B Album and Best R&B Song for "Crazy in Love," her smash single featuring Jay-Z. With her five Grammy wins, Beyoncé tied the record set by Lauryn Hill, Alicia Keys, and Norah Jones for the most Grammys to be won in a single year by a female artist. Most recently, Beyoncé was invited to perform for the nation's highest honor, at the Kennedy Center Honors, in a tribute to Tina Turner. She also has numerous film credits to her name. She displayed her comedic prowess as "Foxxy Cleopatra" in *Goldmember*, starring Mike Myers. Beyoncé also landed a lead role in the film *Pink Panther* and starred in the Academy Award–winning movie *Dreamgirls*. Beyoncé has now ventured into another creative territory: clothing design. She and Tina cofounded the fashion label House of Deréon.

Even before Beyoncé had an arsenal of accomplishments under her belt, Tina said she was never anxious about her development. "Her father was really the one who encouraged her to walk and talk. I let her develop at her own pace." As part of her laid-back approach, Tina didn't have a rigid schedule. "My husband and I read to the kids, but there was never a set time." Asked about whether she let Beyoncé watch television growing up, Tina said it was sometimes on in the background, but that it wasn't ever something that she was drawn to. "Beyoncé wasn't really into television, because she was always running around outside and making up dance routines." Planting the seed for her career as a future fashion designer, Tina encouraged Beyoncé's creativity and love for fashion. "Beyoncé and I would visit consignment shops and buy clothes and then take them home and bead and jewel them and make them into pieces of wearable artwork."

Her creative activities spanned the spectrum, Tina recalled. "When she was younger, my husband and I put her in singing and dancing lessons." But it wasn't because they saw some talent that had to be cultivated. In fact, it was quite the opposite. "We thought it would be a good idea to put her in singing and dancing classes because she was shy." Tina said, however, that she and her husband never forced anything on Beyoncé. "We always talked to her to make sure that it was something she wanted to do and that it was okay if she changed her mind." The only nudging Tina consistently gave Beyoncé was the reminder about having passion for what you do. "We always told her that she could be the best at what she does, but she has to love it first."

As the owner of a beauty salon and a working mom, Tina had to schedule family time; it's not something that would have just happened if left to its own devices. "We would try our best to eat dinner together as a family, but I always set aside time on Saturday, in between my hair appointments, to spend time with my children." Family time at the Knowles house was also centered around religion. "We would go to church at St. John's very regularly," Tina recalled. But religion was also a value Tina lived. "I believed strongly in giving back to the community and would try to do that any chance we got."

Asked about when she saw that Beyoncé had the type of star power that would lead her to become one of the most successful singers in history, Tina said it was actually her dancing instructor, Ms. Darlette, who first noticed Beyoncé's talent. "We caught on when Beyoncé was about five years old and sang solo at a school recital that Ms. Darlette had entered her into. My husband and I sat in the audience totally stunned and it was then that we saw she had this gift." Not only did Tina encourage her daughter with praise, she was an active part of helping Beyoncé take it to the next level. "We let the girls rehearse at our house, I made their costumes, and my husband came on as their manager."

Although most parents usually have to police the social activity during their children's teenage years, Tina said she actually had to put pressure on Beyoncé to be *more* social. "I remember telling her to go to a party or hang out with kids from their school more because Beyoncé was so passionate about singing and dancing that all she wanted to do was rehearse. I wanted to make sure she didn't miss out on being a teenager, so I would encourage her to take a break and go relax with the other kids and have some fun." However, Beyoncé didn't spend all her time at home choreographing dance moves. "We traveled to a lot of places as a family and went to museums." A large part of Beyoncé's unofficial education, Tina said, was the hours she spent at her hair salon. "Beyoncé was always exposed to the daily conversations there, as well as all sorts of hair shows."

By no means does Tina mask her pride in Beyoncé's litany of accomplishments, but she said that her superstar sensation daughter could have been anything that she wanted to be and that would have been fine with her. It's this down-to-earth attitude that she made sure to impart to Beyoncé. "One phrase that I live by is that 'Beauty is only skin deep and that no matter how pretty you are, you still need to be kind, nice, and respectful to the people around you.'"

Tina is quick to say that Beyoncé's success is based on God-given talent. "All my husband and I did was give her love, support, and encouragement that she could do it." Still, she seems to know a thing or two about raising a rock star. "I would just encourage mothers to let their children be themselves, love them for who they are, listen to them, help them believe in themselves, and encourage them to put their best foot forward in all that they do." Perhaps, though, Tina's image of herself of a mother offers the most insight into how Beyoncé has become Beyoncé. "I'm a mother who loves her children and grandson with all her heart and who encourages them to be the best people they can be and to treat others how you would want to be treated."

Marilyn Gentry

Mother of MATT LAUER

"I never kept my children on a schedule."

Given that Matt Lauer has been an integral force in helping the *Today* show reach the impressive milestone of being the second-longest-running television series in the history of broadcasting, it might come as a surprise to some that Marilyn Gentry, mother of the affable anchor, was not the least bit anxious about Matt hitting certain milestones as a child. She has raised a son who has interviewed everyone from President George W. Bush to Alex Rodriguez. Now, married with three children of his own, Matt has won a Daytime Emmy for Outstanding Special Class Program, has been named one of *People* magazine's 50 Most Beautiful People, and has been a guest on just about every major talk show.

Marilyn said even when she did try to encourage development, like when she signed Matt and his older sister, April, up for swimming lessons, she was relaxed about it. "We gave both kids swimming lessons, but neither of them learned. They learned on their own about a year later." As part of her laid-back parenting approach, Marilyn avoided schedules. "I never kept my children on a schedule. I dislike schedules for myself; although I am very organized, but I find schedules are horrific. [The children] never had to eat at a certain time. . . . It wasn't yes, breakfast at a certain time, within an hour, lunch at the same time, within an hour. Dinner was difficult. My husband, my first husband, didn't get home until seven so I usually fed the kids before then. They would sit with us at the table while we ate."

Marilyn said that just being there was one of the things she did "right," and she credited that for helping Matt tap into success. "I always made it a point to be home and not stay out. . . . I wanted to be home with the kids." Even when Marilyn had a job, she found one that accommodated the kids' schedule. "I think I was a good mom because I was there. When I did go to work, I always had a job where I could come home and be home a half hour later than when my kids came home from school."

Marilyn raised Matt in the upper-middle-class suburb of Chappaqua, New York, and gave him a lifestyle to match that community. "We always had plenty and we always lived very well. . . . Matt always had wonderful taste and I guess we indulged the kids. We didn't overly indulge them, but we gave them what they needed and what they wanted." Like family, religion played a central role in Matt's upbringing. "We went to church almost every Sunday."

When it came to the simple stuff, Marilyn was less indulgent. "I was really insistent that they pick up their toys." When it came to disciplining, Marilyn said Richard—her second husband—was the *real* disciplinarian. "I tried to present a unified front with him, even though it was very hard at times." Taking into account Matt's personality, as one who responded to a softer touch, Marilyn would "try to ease up with Matt because Richard was such a strict disciplinarian."

The idyllic, upper-middle-class suburban setting did not shelter Matt from life's hardships. In fact, Marilyn described her relationship with her first husband as "not particularly stable." "It was kind of a cool relationship. That's why I got divorced." A year after her divorce, Marilyn married a man who became the daily father figure for Matt. "Richard was a vital part of Matt's life. . . . He was crazy about children. . . . He really adopted my kids in a very open way." Although Matt never called Richard "Dad," his relationship with his biological father was strained growing up. "His real father got married and wasn't as conscious as he could have been about his children."

Marilyn used her approach of rolling with the punches, and taking life as it comes, with her combined family as well. "On the weekends, I would usually have five children in the house—my two and Richard's three. At that time, we lived in a small garden apartment, but we'd still go on picnics, play tennis, or do something outside."

Marilyn's parenting and life mantra was less about meeting expectations and more about encouraging her children to find something that made them tick. "I always told both of my children to try their best and to find something that they loved to do and it would never seem like work. To find something that they were happy with was much more important." Letting Matt find his own way, with encouragement and the right dose of teasing, was the approach Marilyn used. "We would laugh at him and laugh with him. . . . I think children have to find their own way and they both did and they're both successful."

Starting in early childhood, Matt displayed the skills that would later land him in the anchor chair. "He had a wonderful sense of humor. . . . We laughed a lot with him because he was so entertaining." With the entertainment industry in his DNA—Marilyn was a model and her father, Art Gentry, was a singer—Matt was constantly exposed to people, music, and social activity. "I thought more, though, that he'd be behind the scenes than in front of the camera." Still, Marilyn saw that Matt did have camera presence. "Matt and April would always perform plays when they were little. Matt's father would always say, 'He's going to be something in the business.' And then we just let it go because we knew he would pursue it if he wanted to." But the entertainment business wasn't just in Matt's DNA; growing up, Matt was very exposed to it. "There was always music around because I was in show business and his father was in the business." Making things fun and lively was a big part of how Marilyn parented. "We had all of our friends who were involved in music and every weekend we had wonderful entertainers because all of our friends were in the business. . . . Overall, though, we had a very casual household."

Even when it came to grades and school, Marilyn said she didn't push Matt. "He used to laugh, and we laugh at it now; he says, 'I don't think you ever looked at my report card.' I said, 'I certainly did!' Matt said it took a lot of pressure off him." Growing up in the shadow of an overachieving older sister, Matt was not an academic superstar. "Matt wasn't a great student. My daughter was the wonderful student. We'd check his homework and make sure he certainly got passing grades."

Marilyn was a hands-on parent when it came to sports and socializing—two areas where Matt excelled. "We went to all his games, whatever games he was playing, baseball or football. . . . We knew all of his friends, and all of his girlfriends. We got along great."

Even when Matt went to college, she didn't push him in any direction. "Matt went to school in Ohio and decided to major in communication." Having had the roll-with-the-punches attitude modeled for him his whole life, when Matt didn't get the job he wanted, he went to work as an intern at a West Virginia television station, a job that was a critical stepping-stone in his wildly successful broadcasting career.

For Marilyn, pinpointing the one thing she did exactly "right" was difficult. "I think I just loved him and always told him that God loved him."

Phyllis Stephens
Mother of JOHN LEGEND

"I didn't force him to go any further than he wanted to."

*P*hyllis Stephens, the mother of John Legend, the platinum-selling musician, said she was always praising the Lord when John was young. "I don't know if it was because he always heard me saying it, but his first word was 'hallelujah.'" Today, John has good reason to keep saying his first word. Just shy of his thirtieth birthday, John has already collaborated with some of the biggest names in the business, such as Kanye West, Jay-Z, Lauryn Hill, and Alicia Keys. In 2004, he released his platinum-selling album *Get Lifted* that produced two top 100 songs. Taking a somewhat unusual path for someone who has topped the billboard charts, John first studied at the University of Pennsylvania, on an academic scholarship, where he majored in English with an emphasis on African-American literature and culture. After graduating in 1999, he dabbled in consulting and performed on the nightclub circuit in New York, Philadelphia, and Washington, D.C. John recently launched the Show Me Campaign, an organization that encourages his fans to donate money to help improve living conditions in Ghana. John has appeared in everything from Lexus commercials, to the closing music of Apple CEO Steve Jobs's keynote presentations, to the Live Earth concert in London.

As might be expected from a child whose first word was hallelujah, religion was front and center in John's upbringing. But Phyllis didn't think of religion in traditional terms. "We called it a relationship with Jesus Christ," she said. Religion and regimen were the cornerstones of John's childhood. Reflecting on the roots of her approach, Phyllis said, "I grew up being raised as a disciplined person, so that's how I raised my kids."

John was an early bloomer, Phyllis recalled. "He started walking at around eleven months." What really stood out about John's development, however, was that he responded very fast and talked early. "When he was still in his crib, he was speaking in full sentences."

As a stay-at-home mom, Phyllis didn't have babysitters or put John in nursery school, so she felt it was incumbent on her to take on the role of teacher. "I would always walk around the room and point out everything so John would be able to associate an object with a word." In fact, Phyllis said that her husband made a special seat—a bumper seat—so that John and his brother, whom they affectionately called "Bumper," could see out the window when they were driving places. "Teaching was something I loved to do, and I wanted to help them learn." Elaborating on her hybrid role as parent-teacher, "I was training them to be good people. I felt that this was my project. I wanted to try to teach them everything I knew," Phyllis said. Part of her pedagogy was no television in the house. "I didn't want my kids influenced by the television," Phyllis said, explaining why she enforced this strict policy. "I wanted them to be influenced by us, their parents."

Eventually, though, Phyllis eased up a bit. "We brought it back when John was eleven."

Asked how she was able to straddle the fine line between parent and teacher, Phyllis said it was all about the relationship she had with John. "You know, a lot of parents don't have relationships with their children, but that was my priority. I was there for John, and I think that made him receptive to what I had to teach him." But "being there" certainly didn't mean coddling her son; it meant teaching him responsibility. Phyllis said she was the type of mother who made John walk to school if he missed the bus. "It certainly happened," Phyllis recalled. "And it was a long walk, because we lived on the east end and their school was on the north end."

Although John took a slightly unusual path to the musical success he now enjoys—studying literature at an Ivy League school and working in consulting—music was a staple of his childhood. "The whole family was constantly belting out some kind of tune," Phyllis recollected. "I was always at choir rehearsal." Asked if there was a defining moment when she saw that her son had what it took to become a platinum-selling artist, Phyllis said that she just casually noticed when John was four years old that "he had a good voice." Phyllis said that, just like she did with all of his other talents, she encouraged him. Singing, though, was not enough for John, so he took up the piano. "Per usual, John was a sensation. The piano teacher was so impressed with him because he was a four-year-old who was able to sing the songs as he was reading the music," Phyllis said.

Even though he was a star piano student, John decided, when he was eleven, to give up piano lessons. Phyllis never pushed him to continue taking piano lessons. "I knew he had reached his threshold with it. I never forced him to do anything." In fact, Phyllis did everything she could to facilitate John following the beat of his *own* drummer. "When he was younger I put him in a boys' choir that sang at places like Cincinnati Reds games. John decided he didn't want to be in the choir anymore, so I had to break the contract and pay some money to get him out. Whenever he didn't like something, I responded to that. I didn't ever force him to go any further than he wanted to." For some, decisions like giving up piano lessons and dropping out of a prestigious choir might have meant an abrupt halt to an otherwise burgeoning music career. John was different, though. "It didn't matter that he wasn't taking lessons. My best friend said this about John, and I think it captures him so poignantly. 'God put music in John. He is a songwriter and all he has to do is let it come out of him.' At nine years old, she just saw it in him." Phyllis said her best friend wasn't the only person who saw something remarkable in him. She did as well. "I remember right after my mother passed away, the choir director needed a song, so John got on the piano and taught the missionary his song. So there we were, this big, old choir of women, singing a song a nine-year-old boy had taught us."

Reflecting on the role she has played helping John become "the John Legend," Phyllis said she believes that the biggest gift she gave to John—yes, even more than the piano lessons—was her time. "The quality time I gave Johnny is what I would say shaped him in the formative years of his life." Boiling down the image she has of herself as a mother, Phyllis said it's a trifecta: "I'm a nurturer, I'm an encourager, and I'm interested in everything my kids do."

Helene Shalotsky

Mother of DR. ROBI LUDWIG

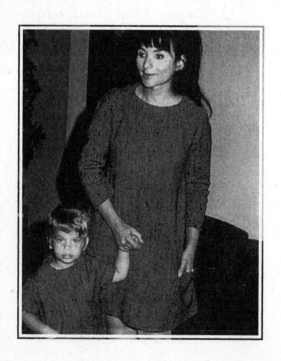

"Children may not always seem to do what you say, but they always seem to imitate what you *do*."

$\mathcal{H}$elene Shalotsky, the mother of Dr. Robi Ludwig, the nationally known psychotherapist and award-winning reporter, said her mother—Robi's grandmother—was always easy to talk to and became Helene's confidante growing up. Since it worked for her, Helene took this same approach with her daughter, Robi, who has gone on to become a professional confidante. Robi is a regular contributor on shows such as *Larry King*, *Today*, and *Nancy Grace*, helping guests understand their damaged relationships. Also on the TV front, Robi is the host of two shows: *One Week to Save a Marriage* and GSN's *Without Prejudice?* Venturing into a variety of media outlets, Robi was recently made a contributing editor to *Cookie* magazine, a modern lifestyle magazine for mothers. Before becoming a celebrity, Robi worked as a social rehabilitation counselor for patients with severe psychiatric problems. She is also the author of *Till Death Do Us Part: Love, Marriage, and the Mind of the Killer Spouse*. Robi is married with two children.

Growing up, Robi's strong ethical and moral groundings were shaped by religion. Helene said spirituality played a daily part in Robi's childhood. "We had Shabbat dinners each Friday night. We lit candles and said prayers. . . . We kept a kosher home, the kids went to Hebrew school, and all the Jewish holidays were celebrated." Having these religious rituals fostered a family togetherness that was the heart of Robi's childhood. "As a family, we'd also go to Broadway shows, museums, restaurants, synagogue events, and sporting events."

As the child of immigrants, Helene said that her background growing up influenced how she raised her three daughters. "Since my parents worked to give us an education, I wanted to build on that and give my children even more. We wanted to give them the paradigm of the American Dream: the loving, educated family; the warm, small town; the private college education. . . . Our aim was for our girls to have a happy life; to say that our children were our life would be a most accurate statement." Having seen her parent's strong work ethic modeled for her, Helene said she worked straight through her pregnancy as a New York City schoolteacher. "After Robi was born, I continued to teach part-time during her first eleven years."

Some say raising children is a labor of love, but for Helene raising children was just about the love. "Raising my children was really a total pleasure. I enjoyed every minute." Having a partnership with her husband—a marriage that has spanned over four decades—was a crucial component of this approach. "I really did everything along with my husband," Helene said. When reflecting on the role her relationship with her husband played in parenting such a successful daughter, Helene said it was "paramount." "My husband and I loved each other, liked each other, and respected each other." That, perhaps more than anything, set the tone for Robi's childhood. "By the time the girls came along, we were already a unit and the girls just added more joy and consistency to our family."

Instead of pressuring Robi, Helene just welcomed each development stage enthusiastically. "She crawled at six months, walked at twelve months, and talked fluently by two. . . . It was like having a new doll at each stage." To encourage her development, Helene read a lot of Dr. Seuss books to Robi. Helene wasn't fanatical about the television and said that it was always on in the background. "We watched together." She did a variety of other activities with Robi, too—everything from playing Candy Land to just sitting on the floor and playing informally. "I was a great believer in creative play emanating from a child. . . . However, if I believed I had something to teach them, I led. If they were very motivated to initiate something, they led."

While who "led" and who "followed" changed, Helene stressed that whatever she was doing, she gave it her complete focus. "I would either be playing with Robi on the floor, or overseeing what she was doing. I didn't believe I could concentrate on reading or a phone conversation as well as watch my child. My child always came first."

When it came to the bigger picture, Helene's parenting philosophy included the belief that children should enjoy a spectrum of experiences. As such, she enrolled Robi in tennis, ballet, swimming, and team sports. These activities, combined with Helene's extensive networks of friends, gave Robi a built-in social circle as a child. "My friends are lifelong friends that all my girls know very well. Each holiday season our girls send them all season's greetings." However, being social and outgoing didn't just happen by accident; Helene said she definitely actively cultivated this aspect of Robi's life.

Robi's success is no accident, either. Helene had high expectations for Robi, but instead of vocalizing them, she tried to parent by example. "My husband and I knew that children may not always seem to do what you say, but they always seem to imitate what you *do*, so we simply lived our beliefs: hard work, educational accomplishments, family gatherings for all the holidays and birthdays, vacations to fun family spots, inclusion of friends in family festivities, and showing the love and affection we all felt for each other all the time."

As someone who found so much joy in parenting, it's no surprise that Helene described her parenting style as nurturing. "I just always believed my children were wonderful and a joy to be with because, indeed they were, are." However, she was focused about encouragement and doled it out very pointedly. "I would zoom in on their unique gifts faster than a dog with a bone. A specific kindness was applauded, a well-written thank-you note was extolled." In addition to monitoring the good, Helene was also adept at handling the rocky patches. "When things went awry, I let them know they could fix it and make it better," a quality that Robi has run with in her professional career. "I let them know that when their world got difficult, they knew home would always be their supportive haven."

Helene's mantra to Robi was "This is a gift you'll be giving to yourself" when she was helping her think things through and make choices. "I wanted to instill in them [her children] that some of the things one does are because it's a benefit to your future happiness." Even so, there were times when Helene pushed, particularly in terms of education. "When it came to school, I pushed, and I pushed hard. My family values and teacher standards were very important to me and thus I projected that onto my children." When Helene boiled it down, she thought her parenting tenets were being "a loving, supportive, enthusiastically affectionate parent who offered her children infinite love." It's no surprise that Robi has made a career trying to help people bring the same qualities into their lives and relationships.

Gladys Blunden

Mother of JOAN LUNDEN

"'Can't' is not part of our vocabulary."

*G*ladys Blunden, the mother of former *Good Morning America* icon, television celebrity, and author Joan Lunden, said she always made sure that Joan knew how to talk to adults, a skill that certainly paid off in Joan's wildly successful broadcasting career. "The kids always had to participate and talk with adults," Gladys said. In addition to cultivating their *literal* verbal skills, Joan said her mother imparted the most important language rule of all: "She told us that 'can't' is not part of our vocabulary." Taking this advice to the extreme, Joan has received numerous honors, including, among dozens of others, the Spirit of Achievement Award from Albert Einstein College, the YWCA Outstanding Woman's Speaker Award, and the National Women's Political Caucus Award; and in 1982 she was selected as the Outstanding Mother of the Year for her dedication to motherhood. Today, she is married and the mother of seven.

Joan, the oldest of two, was raised more like a twin with her brother, Jeffery. "I was adopted so we were only seven months and twenty-nine days apart," Jeffery said. Gladys, who was raised in a low-income family, said she wanted "to give her kids everything that she didn't get." As part of that goal, Joan said, her mother always pushed them to expand their horizons—something she certainly modeled in her own life. In addition to showcasing all these lofty qualities—aspiration, motivation, and reaching for the stars—Joan described her mother as someone who just knew how to have a good time. "She was this vivacious woman who always played the piano and got the kids singing in the house and really kept things going."

It was no secret that Gladys had high expectations for her daughter. "I would say to her, 'You can go any place that you want to go.' I told her it was possible for her to achieve anything she wanted." Joan said she definitely internalized this approach. "My mother's style of parenting was obvious. There was an underlying atmosphere and assumption that we would always live to be the pillars of our community." Speaking more candidly, Joan said, "It was quietly known that you were expected not just to be a housewife, or a spoiled brat."

Joan displayed signs of being an entertainer from the time she was six, and Gladys encouraged her on this path. "I remember when Joan was taking dance classes and I bought a convertible hardtop. I put a board over the whole interior so Joan could do her dancing on top of the car. She was always leading the parade."

Gladys described her parenting style as "involved" when it came to both Joan's academic and social life. "I belonged to the PTA. . . . I was very friendly with all of her friends. I let her entertain at home, so that I knew what was going on." In recalling her mother's involvement in her life, and the community, Joan said she was "very involved." "My mom would take us to school every morning and pick us up every afternoon. . . . She was very involved in the Sacramento Medical Auxiliary . . . she was always involved socially." As far as discipline was concerned, Gladys said she and her husband presented a unified front with their children. In describing her mother's disciplinary style, Joan says, "We didn't live in a strict house at all."

Gladys didn't have to do much prodding when it came to helping Joan achieve. "When she was in third grade, she was doing fifth-grade work." A believer in "hands-on" education, Gladys said she was the type of parent who would pull her kids out of school for a day "to go see something special." As part of this approach, when Joan was just sixteen, Gladys enrolled her in an exchange program in Mexico City to immerse her in a different set of experiences. "She lived with a Mexican family so she could see what life was like down there."

Exposure to different ideas, cultures, and religions was a critical component of Joan's upbringing. Joan described being raised with an openness to many religions. "We had a babysitter who was Catholic and every now and then we'd go to church; my best friends were the Kleins, so sometimes I'd go to synagogue with them. . . . You might say I had a very ecumenical upbringing due to the desire on my mother's part not to have any disagreement in the house about religion."

Continuing on her path of academic accomplishment, Joan completed twelfth grade at sixteen. When she encountered some resistance from her high school about letting her graduate so early, Joan said her mom came in and pushed. "They finally acquiesced." When it came to Joan's education, Gladys always took on a very active role. "My mom found out about a school called World Campus Afloat, where you went to college on a ship and traveled around the world, and she actually took my college essay from the other schools and attached it. I got accepted."

Gladys had a clear motivation for wanting Joan to attend World

Campus Afloat. Joan recalled, "She said to me, 'I think you need to get out of this area, where none of your friends have the same aspirations as you do, and I think you need to go out and find out what a big, wide world this is and how much it has to offer because you want to do more.'" Gladys made a conscious effort to push her kids beyond their comfort zone, or as she put it, "exposing them to all things that were available to them rather than just letting them play at home with their tiddledywinks." "I wanted them to get out into the world to see what it had to offer." Gladys said she was able to push Joan out of her comfort zone because of the underlying faith she had in her. "I always trusted Joan's outlook on everything, so I let her try anything."

When Joan was twelve, her family's life was altered forever after her father tragically died in a plane crash. "From that time on our lives changed drastically," Joan said. "My mom had to figure out how to replace the tears in her eyes with dollar signs. She had to figure out how to make it, because we were still young and there were many years ahead of us." Like mother like daughter. They picked themselves—and each other—up and moved forward. "I remember my mother saying, 'I can't just sit around and mope around. I've got to get out there and be strong. . . . She went to real-estate school and became a Realtor. . . . She also had to take care of my father's medical practice." Joan said that seeing this kind of tenacity from her mother "made me not afraid to push the limits," even though, as she put it, "I was given enough rope that I clearly could have hung myself." Reflecting on it today, Joan said coping with her father's death was an important—albeit excruciatingly painful—building block to her success. "I think that being affected by a trauma like that made me become a survivor, and what an incredible quality to have if you're going to be successful."

Seeing how her mother handled her father's death taught Joan two important lessons: one, that you have to get back on the horse and, two, that there are no safety nets in life. "After what happened to me, you realize that safety can be taken away at any moment in time, unpredictably, so you better be able to take care of yourself." Passing on the hard-earned wisdom and upbeat attitude to the next generation of women in her family, Joan said, "I have tried to impart my mother's positive attitude, and the sense that failure is not an option. I've always said to my daughters, 'When you eliminate failure as an option, your chances for success are infinitely better.'"

Having a mother like Gladys, who always pushed the limits and saw what more could be done, made eliminating failure much more doable. When Joan started a successful modeling agency, her mother recognized further potential. Joan recalled her mom saying, "I think it's really wonderful that you're helping guide all these young girls and that you're getting them jobs in modeling, but if you put half of the effort into making yourself a star, as you're putting into them, then *you'd* become a star." And so, on her mother's advice, Joan did.

Kathy Mazur

Mother of KEVIN MAZUR

"If you fall down, dust yourself off, and start all over again."

Although Kathy Mazur—the mother of photographer-to-the-rock-stars Kevin Mazur—thought her son would become a professional athlete, she was the one who bought him his first 35mm camera, a gift that helped set in motion Kevin's rise to the top of his field. Today, Kevin photographs the biggest stars in the music industry. Insiders say that his success hinges not only on his talent but on his equipment, the first piece of which was bought by his mother!

Kevin has been onstage with Madonna, in the recording studio with Bob Dylan, and on tour with the Rolling Stones. He regularly shoots some of the biggest events in the music industry, including Woodstock, the Rock and Roll Hall of Fame Induction Ceremony, and the MTV and VH1 Music Awards. He is the founder of WireImage, the leading provider of entertainment, sports, and news imagery. Kevin has also ventured into book publishing, a project that will benefit Save the Music, a nonprofit organization dedicated to saving instrumental music in public schools. Kevin has two children.

Kathy, who was raised in a low-income household, said she tried to give her three children—Kevin and his two younger sisters, Maureen and Kerri—everything she didn't have. "I never said 'no' to my children." Growing up, Kathy said they were a close family. "After my father died, Kevin's grandmother, my mother, came to live with us. . . . Kevin was really the apple of her eye."

Since Kevin was her first child, Kathy described an excitement about seeing him reach certain milestones. "He did everything so early," she recalled. "He was eight months old when he climbed out of the crib." While Kathy said that after the third child, she grew to hate the nursery rhymes and Dr. Seuss books, Kevin's place in the birth order, as the oldest, meant that he got to hear all the stories. "I used to read all the nursery rhymes and books to him at night before he went to bed."

Describing herself as "the typical suburban mom," Kathy said she belonged to the PTA and enrolled Kevin in the Boy Scouts and Little League. However, the attention she paid to Kevin was hardly typical. "When he started competitive diving, I had to drive twenty miles to take him for lessons." In addition to encouraging his athletic talents and interests, Kathy said she always imparted the importance of going to college. "I wanted him to have a secure career."

Characterizing her family as a "huggy and kissy" one, Kathy said that while she was affectionate, she tried to tone it down in front of Kevin's friends. More than anything, she emphasized the value she placed on being together. "We ate dinner together every night. . . . We spent weekends together." Even as Kevin got older, the family still did things together. "When the kids were in their teens, we bought a camper. We even went cross-country to Mt. Rushmore!" As Kathy put it, "My interests were the kids." Kathy credited her forty-seven years of marriage to her husband as the crux of her tight-knit family.

Falling somewhere between the extremes of totally lenient and ironfisted, Kathy said she would ground Kevin if he got in trouble. Although Kathy was the more involved parent—her husband was a firefighter who sometimes worked two jobs—they still managed to present a unified front when it came to discipline.

When it came to school, Kathy wanted Kevin to get good grades, but she also rolled with the punches when he decided not to make school a priority. "In junior high Kevin told me it wasn't cool to be smart. . . . Once he flunked something and had to go to summer school. That was it. He never went to summer school again." But that incident was hardly reflective of Kevin's work ethic. In fact, Kathy described Kevin as having a very strong work ethic, something she helped to cultivate and encourage. "He was a lifeguard every summer from the time he was sixteen. Sometimes he had three jobs."

Although some mothers might have discouraged their teenage sons from sneaking into concerts and taking pictures, Kathy said she thought, if he was going to do it, Kevin should at least have a good camera. "I bought him a camera for high school graduation." As she described it, there was no turning back for Kevin from that point. "He went to college to study art and design, and then went to St. John's to study photography. He dropped out his senior year, and I wasn't happy." Still, Kathy always told Kevin that he should try anything and not be afraid of failure.

Looking back on how her parenting style impacted Kevin, Kathy credited her philosophy of "If you fall down, dust yourself off, and start all over again," a lesson Kevin certainly internalized and applied to his professional life. "Kevin lost his business, and then started all over again. I always told him to try anything and not be afraid." Asked about what she thinks she did to help Kevin get where he is today, she said, "I always encouraged him, and I always thought that he could succeed."

Madeline McElveen

Mother of BONNIE McELVEEN

"Whatever voice you use with your children, they are going to use it back to you. If you push them around when they are young, they will shove you around when they are older. You have to show them love in the way you want to be shown love."

Madeline McElveen—the mother of Bonnie McElveen, the chairwoman of the American Red Cross—said her pregnancy with Bonnie, the oldest of her three children, was a difficult one. "I just prayed to God and asked him to deliver me a normal baby. It was really a record birth. She was a miracle then and she has been a miracle ever since." And that's no exaggeration. Bonnie was appointed chairwoman of the American Red Cross by President George W. Bush in 2004. Bonnie was also the former U.S. ambassador to Finland and the CEO and owner of Pace Communications, Inc., the largest private custom-publishing company in the United States. As the U.S. ambassador to Finland, Bonnie led several initiatives to success, including the Helsinki Women Business Leaders Summit, Stop Child Trafficking: End Modern-Day Slavery, and Children of Karelia. The program helped Finnish and Russian charities assist children at risk for drugs, crime, HIV/AIDS, and trafficking. For her exceptional and outstanding services, Bonnie was awarded one of Finland's highest honors—the Commander Grand Cross of the Order of the Lion. She also received the Dr. Carl-Christian Rosenbröijer Award. Previous honorees were former president George H. W. Bush and Dr. Henry Kissinger. Bonnie now lives in Greensboro, North Carolina, with her husband, Bynum Merritt Hunter, an attorney in the law firm of Smith Helms Mulliss & Moore. They have a twenty-one-year-old son.

Madeline described her own parents, Bonnie's grandparents, as "very much in love." She went on to explain that her upbringing was rooted in deep faith. "Church was the center of our life. We went to church on Wednesday and Sunday." Asked about her economic status growing up, Madeline said, "We were rich in everything except finances." Using her approach that "every moment is a teachable moment," she and her husband taught Bonnie the value of money early on. "I saw her whole life as a learning experience. I used to take her shopping and explain things to her. She was like a little adult to me." So instead of leaving Bonnie at home when she and her husband went to "adult" functions, Madeline said they would take her with them. "Bonnie was mostly around adults growing up."

Expressing the same passion and drive that has gotten Bonnie where she is today, Madeline said she was twenty-seven before she married, because she was so involved in her career as a teacher. "I was having such a wonderful time teaching school. I was not in a hurry. I just thoroughly enjoyed what I was doing." Motherhood, then, became an extension of teaching. As a teacher, Madeline did everything she could to impart her deep love of scholarship and knowledge to her children. "I knew in my heart that children learned in the womb. . . . I also think that if you put anything to music, children can learn it. I put a tape recorder in their crib with the ABCs and 123s." But more than just feeding knowledge to her children, Madeline believed that she taught so successfully because of her enthusiasm for and commitment to the process. "You have to feed knowledge into your children, and you have to enjoy learning yourself," she said.

Madeline said she always seized moments and opportunities, so when her husband got stationed in Germany, there was no question as to whether she would move there with her two young children. Reflecting on this decision today, she said, "I was so superbly happy just to have the opportunity to travel." Besides, she believes there are no accidents. "We had such a foundation in faith. We thought everything happened for a purpose and we loved opportunities. Our family was godly, so we never looked at it as a strain or a stress. . . . Back then, we didn't even know what the word *stress* meant."

Although Madeline believed that every moment was a teachable moment, TV did not fall into that category. "I didn't believe in TV or radio. When we were driving, I never allowed my husband to turn on the radio. I think so often adults turn on the radio and tune out the children." In a poignant example of how Madeline took advantage of every opportunity, when she taught her children how to cross the street, she did so not by saying, " 'Hold my hand, I don't want you to get run over.' . . . Instead I said, 'Take my hand and please take me across the street, because I can't see as well as you.' And then I said, 'Thank you. What would I have ever done without you?' " It was also Madeline's conviction that you cannot praise your children enough. "It makes them more secure in life."

Madeline has, in fact, created a whole movement around squelching negativity. "It's called the 'Shhh club.' The great thing is that before you say anything to your child, you say, 'Shhh,' if you think something negative is going to come out. Don't ever tear down your child, build them up." Rooting it all in her faith, she said, "My saying is always, 'This is a day that God has made. Let's rejoice. Let's see who can jump out of bed first.' "

These ideals, morals, and values hardly existed in a vacuum. They had a tangible impact on how Bonnie related to the world. "When Bonnie was in the first grade, and the teacher would criticize another student, she would get up to sharpen her pencil, but she was really going by the student to let him or her know that everything was going to be okay." Explaining how this all came about, Madeline explained, "I taught my kids to love God, and when you love God, you love people. You don't look for their faults; you look for their potential, and realize we are all here to help each other."

Madeline was full of wisdom and always liked to couple her lessons with hands-on ways her children could relate to what could be abstract concepts for children. "I remember we talked about the word *can't*, and I said, 'Why don't we just take the word *can't* and bury it.' So we had a funeral. We had the kids write the word and we dug a hole in the backyard and we put it in the ground. I just wanted them to know that with God's help we can do anything."

Madeline said that her approach to parenting and her approach to discipline are both rooted in love. "I correct with love. . . . I never disciplined any of my children in front of anyone else. There is a special place in your house for that. I spanked my children and I told them it was because 'I wanted everyone else to love you as much as I love you, and people do not love naughty children.' " As a result, "When I said something, I only said it once."

A believer in "what goes around comes around," Madeline had a keen awareness of *how* she spoke to her children. "I think whatever voice you use with your children, they are going to use it back to you. If you push them around when they are young, they will shove you around when they are older. You have to show them love in the way you want to be shown love." Attributing it all to a positive attitude,

Madeline said, "I think you have to say to them, 'You are going to be the best today.'" Touching back on her teachable moments philosophy, Madeline's practical advice to mothers is: "When you walk up the steps, teach them to add, when you are walking down, use it as a lesson in subtraction." For Madeline, motherhood is encompassed in just one simple word—a word she said describes the image of herself as a parent—*godly*.

Betty Trimble

Mother of TIM McGRAW

"The straight-up truth is the best policy."

Elizabeth Ann Trimble, better known as Betty—the mother of one of the most famous country singers of all time, Tim McGraw—said that while she was pregnant she prayed that her baby would be someone special. Today, she says, "God answers prayers," even though "special" is an understatement in light of all that Tim has accomplished. Tim released his first album in 1992 and had his first major hit in 1994 with *Not a Moment Too Soon*, which sold over five million copies, topped the Billboard 200 and the country album charts, and won him an Academy of Country Music Award. Every album since has built on this success, going multiplatinum, reaching the top five on the Billboard 200, and culling honors and awards. Tim is married to country music star Faith Hill with whom he often collaborates by creating hits like "It's Your Love" for Tim's *Everywhere* album, as well as touring in the Live 8: The Long Walk to Justice concert series. Tim and Faith founded the Neighbor's Keeper Foundation, which provides funding for communities in need. In 2002, Tim helped the American Red Cross unveil its first-ever National Celebrity Cabinet. Tim and Faith have three daughters.

Although Betty said she didn't push Tim to pursue a career in music, she described her own affinity for it. "I loved music and I would get up and dance and pretend I was doing it for him," Betty said. Living in "the boonies," as Betty put it, meant that she had to create activities. "I'd invite all the kids over all the time, and then kids started gravitating toward our house. I just figured if I had stuff to do at my house, it kept them busy. It kept them out of trouble." Harkening back to a different time when there weren't as many distractions and people had to create their own entertainment, Betty described going for walks and having picnics at the house. "I made curtains for a stage and would have the kids dancing and doing stuff. I was always interacting with my children. I spent all my time with them. In fact, there was hardly ever another adult around." Understanding that they "grow up so fast," Betty said she felt an urgency to be with Tim as much as possible. "I just felt like I should play with him whenever he was around." Betty would even turn off the TV when Tim came into the room, so she could focus her undivided attention on him.

Encouragement was a staple of Betty's parenting strategy. "I just always told them, 'If you want to do something, you can do it.' When Tim was old enough to understand, I would tell him, 'If you want to do it try it, just give it a shot.'" Betty said that she always tried to frame failure as a product of not trying. "I always told Tim, 'A failure is someone who doesn't try, and just sits back.'" It was these simple words of encouragement that Betty credited for helping her son get over important childhood and adult hurdles. "I remember he wanted to play basketball, but he really didn't know how to play. I told him, 'That's what school is about. If you don't know how to play, the coach will teach you how to play.' He ended up really loving basketball."

Betty also spoke up at other crucial junctures in Tim's life, providing the moral and emotional support for Tim to follow his dream of becoming a singer. "When Tim wanted to pursue his singing career, I encouraged him, even though he was in his third year of college. I said, 'Go for it, son. You don't have any responsibilities. You don't have a house to pay for. You're not married. You don't have kids. Go for it now while you don't have any responsibilities. School will always be there, and if you don't make it, at least you tried.' So that's what he did."

But more than just verbally encouraging Tim's goals, Betty said she took concrete actions to further her son's pursuits. "I made sure he had a basketball hoop at my house, when I could finally afford it. I saved up money just so he could have it." She said that although they were poor, Tim never felt like they didn't have a lot of money because "I always tried to give them what I could. Tim always said he felt richer because I always made sure we had things. And if he wanted a pair of Nikes or something that was expensive, I told him I'd save up until I could get it."

Having to tell Tim what happened to his father, who did not want to be involved in Tim's life and instead wanted to pursue his baseball career, was another pivotal moment for Betty as a mother. Believing that the straight-up truth was the best policy, Betty said, "I told him as much of the story as I could. He just looked at me and was crying and said, 'Tug McGraw, the baseball player, is my dad? Does he know about me?' And I said, 'Yes, he knows about you, but he chose a career that made it hard for him to be a father.'" She said she then did everything in her power to try and reunite Tim with his father, after her son expressed a deep desire to meet him. "I called Tug. I was nervous about calling him, but I did." Even with an absent father, Betty described a normalcy and routine to Tim's childhood. "I read to him a lot. Even though he couldn't understand it, he just liked the sound of his mamma's voice. So he'd lay there like he was listening."

Drawing from the things that she didn't like about her own childhood, Betty said she made a concerted effort to be more affectionate than her mother. "The one thing my mother didn't do when I was little was hug us and say 'I love you.' So from the time Tim was born, I started doing that." Betty did, however, pass on other parts of her upbringing to Tim. "I made sure to teach the children something about Italian culture . . . we did a lot of Italian cooking. And Tim is a very good cook."

Growing up in a small town meant that Tim had the opportunity to stand out at an early age. "Tim had his first solo in the church choir group when he was three." Religion and the church were always a central part of Tim's upbringing. "He loved religion. He loved me to read him stories out of the Bible when he was little. I think it's because he loves history and we always said he was going to be a preacher. . . . He loved reading the Bible and listening to those stories. As a teenager, he could go head-to-head with our preacher playing Bible trivia." Though it was clear that Tim had real musical talent, Betty didn't try to make him pursue a musical career. "I always encouraged him, but I didn't try to make him do. I didn't want to force him into things like my mother did with me."

Asked about how Tim survived all the hardship in his life—growing up poor and with an absent father—Betty said, "I just listened to my kids, and I always told them that they could come talk to me about anything and most of the time they did." Despite all their challenges, Betty emphasized living life to the fullest—an approach Tim has certainly internalized. "I'd always say to Tim, 'If that is what you want to do, you just got to do it. You've got to live it. You've got to eat it. You've got to breathe it. That's what you've got to work for.'"

Most important, Betty said her approach to parenting was defined by not pushing or prodding. "One thing I never did is push Tim. I saw those mothers who miss the boat at being a beauty queen, and then they push their kids to be beauty queens. It's got to be what your child wants. And everybody says, 'So *you* pushed him toward music,' when they heard I was interested in music. I did not. I really didn't." Asked about her summation of herself as a parent, Betty said she saw her role in her children's lives as a synthesis: "I was their teacher and their mother."

Doris Paulsin

Mother of GEORGETTE MOSBACHER

"We were all in this together. One for all and all for one."

*D*oris Paulsin, the mother of Georgette Mosbacher, the president and CEO of Borghese, a global cosmetics company, said she used to tell her daughter, "We're searching for beauty everywhere we go." Ironically, Georgette has found both the metaphorical beauty her mother was referring to and an actual career in the industry. In addition to being CEO of Borghese, Georgette is a Republican National Committeewoman for New York State, and the founder of the Children's Advocacy Center of Manhattan. She is also the author of several books, including *Feminine Force*—a motivational guide for women—and *It Takes Money, Honey*—a woman's guide to financial freedom. Mosbacher has been featured on numerous radio and television shows as well as in *Forbes*, *BusinessWeek*, *Time*, and *Vogue* magazines.

Doris said that birth order played a large role in shaping the upbringing of Georgette, who was the oldest of four children. "She had the bulk of responsibilities." In fact, Doris described "responsibility" as the cardinal tenet of her parenting philosophy. "I taught them that we were all in this together, and we were going to all help each other . . . one of us was responsible for what the other person did. . . . It was like one for all and all for one." Raised in a long lineage of strong women, Doris said that her communal approach was imparted to her from her grandmother.

Personal responsibility was paramount in the household where Georgette was raised, and she learned from a young age what takes many people years to internalize: "if you do something bad, we're all going to suffer." By the same token, Doris said she also stressed the positive side—if you make it: "you are making it for your brother, your two sisters, and for me." As a corollary, Doris said she instilled in her children that "We are on this planet for the sole purpose of trying to help others," a value that Georgette certainly lives her life by today with all of her charitable involvement.

Growing up, Georgette displayed the leadership qualities—taking responsibility, executing tasks flawlessly, and maintaining control of a group—that would take her to the helm of a company: "When I was away from the kids, Georgette was in control. She was the mother. She saw to it that everything that I would have done was done. She was unbelievable."

Although the "big picture" stuff, such as cultivating personal responsibility, was important to Georgette's upbringing, so was the smaller stuff. "She had tennis, swimming, and ballet lessons. . . . She loved her dancing. . . . I wanted to expose her to different things. If she wanted to play tennis, she could play tennis. If she wanted to ride a horse, she could." Still, Doris kept her focus on Georgette's talents and interests. "Georgette's passion was drama." Doris, however, did more than just sign Georgette up for drama lessons—she became actively involved with Georgette's interest in theater. "I became the director, and I would put the children in certain parts. When the play was over they would all come to my house, and we'd have an after-play party."

Doris definitely saw something special in Georgette growing up, namely the quality that is an integral ingredient to success: aspiration. "I saw something in Georgette. One day she caught me in a dime store, and she saw a cardboard chest. She wanted it so badly and I thought, 'You know, what do you need that for? You've got a chest.' She took the chest home and she just loved the drawers. One was diamonds. One was pearls. And she'd say, 'Mother, I have to practice because when I grow up they are going to be real.'" While Georgette was certainly shooting for the stars, Doris said she always kept her children grounded with the message that success was not just about personal gratification. "I always said to them, 'We're helping one another because one day one of us may need a lot of help or something, so we have to be successful so we can support each other."

Raising her children as a single mother—Doris's husband passed away when Georgette was young—magnified the responsibility the family felt to each other and shaped how Doris approached parenting. "We didn't have a father, so I had to prepare the children for anything that should befall us." In line with her parenting approach of instilling the lofty lessons of life in addition to the basics, Doris ingrained respect into Georgette, sometimes even using role playing as a teaching tool. "I'd say, 'Now think that is Mr. So-and-so from next door. Now, how are you going to greet him?' . . . I told the children, 'The most important thing is to be honest and say your shoes look pretty, your hair looks nice, and you have a nice apron. You say something honestly and then run on and have a good time.'"

Even though Georgette would go on to control millions of dollars as CEO of a large company, she was raised with very little. As Doris said, "I knew nothing about money." But as an aspiring cosmetics and fashion mogul, Georgette had a good eye from a young age. "Every once in a while Georgette would say, 'I want a Jenson sweater,' or 'I want a certain kind of name brand shoes.' I'd say, 'OK, everybody in the car.' Because we lived in the poor side of town, I'd tell them, 'You're lucky you even have a sweater, but we can work toward getting a Jenson sweater.' " Instead of sheltering Georgette from the "have mores" of the world, Doris exposed her to it. It was all part of the belief that "you can get anything you want, provided you work for it."

Doris described, too, how she openly communicated with her children about financial trade-offs. "Someone would say, 'I want a new bike.' I'd say, 'OK, we'll get you a new bike, but you know what? Right now all we can really afford is new carpeting, and if we get new carpeting, that is something we can all enjoy. So do you mind if we got new carpeting before we get the bike, and we'll get the bike next time?' " Still, Doris exposed Georgette to as much as she possibly could. "From the opera to horseback riding, I wanted to show her that she could have anything that she wanted. . . . I think that was my big message to Georgette, if you want to have front seats at the opera house, you can someday, even if you are sitting in the back row today."

The death of a father and a husband could, and often does, splinter a family. When Georgette's sister, Lynn, reflected about their childhood, she said their mother gave them the power to move through such a difficult period. "A lot of mothers would have given up on their kids. I mean it happens every day. . . . At the funeral I heard someone say, 'I don't think she is going to keep all those children, they might have to be separated; she might have to put them in an orphanage.' Georgette was never the same after that. . . . Georgette then made her mission in life to never ever let this family be separated ever. . . . I remember she took us three younger kids into a room and said to all of us, 'We are in this together. I will never let them separate us.' "

However, it's a fine line, as Lynn pointed out, between the fear and power these traumatic events can instill in you. Crediting her mother, Lynn said, "I think that Georgette gained power through fear." Summing up how she raised four children as a single parent in less than ideal circumstances, Doris said, "It was just about letting them know that you are in charge and that your decisions are only given through love."

Rose Neeleman

Mother of DAVID NEELEMAN

"It is important that children work with you,
instead of telling them what to do."

ose Neeleman is the mother of JetBlue Airways founder
David Neeleman, who has used his three-prong strategy
of low fares, friendly service, and free snacks to take Jet-
Blue into the coveted position of the *third* busiest airline in the
country. JetBlue was also rated the "Best Domestic Airline" by *Condé
Nast Traveler*'s 2003 Readers Choice Awards. David's upbringing is
apparent in every aspect of how he runs his business, from letting
his reservationists work at home to the limitless snacks.

David's career in the airline industry began in 1984 when he
cofounded a low-fare carrier called Morris Air. As president of
Morris Air, David implemented the industry's first electronic tick-
eting system and pioneered a home reservationist system that is

now the hallmark of JetBlue Airways' unique call center: all calls to JetBlue's reservation number are handled by reservationists working out of their homes.

In 1999, David decided the time was right to bring his successful airline formula—innovative, high-quality service plus low fares equals a strong and loyal market—to one of the country's largest aviation markets, New York City, by creating JetBlue Airways. David lives with his wife, Vicki, and their nine children in New Canaan, Connecticut.

David, the second of seven, and born to a mother who was one of nine, was raised in a long lineage of tradition. "My family came over before the *Mayflower* and joined the church the first year it organized. So our grandchildren are actually the ninth generation of the church, which is very unusual," Rose said. Carrying on the tradition of large families, David is now married and has nine of his own children.

As a large family, however, they were anything but disparate. "We're a family that was together a lot. We had a lot of interactions with both my parents and my husband's parents." David was raised in a middle-class neighborhood, even though Rose's family lived in a more affluent area. Content with what she had, Rose said she was "happy being middle class."

Growing up surrounded by his extended family, David fostered close relationships not only with his parents and siblings but also with his grandparents. In fact, David rebuilt his grandfather's grocery store, the store where he worked as a young teenager. "He has also bought the ranch of his other grandfather. It's quite touching the way he's done these two projects to keep up the tradition of his grandfathers."

Growing up in a religious Mormon community, the Neelemans spent time in Brazil as part of a mission for the church. "My husband had been a Mormon missionary in Brazil, and when he came home, the United Press International hired him back as the foreign correspondent. . . . He promised that we'd only be gone for two years. We were gone seven years and yet we really did love it there." The church was central to David's upbringing, not only for the spiritual guidance it offered, but also because of the confidence it helped cultivate, the confidence that would be crucial in his career as an entrepreneur and CEO. "At church, the children would give these little talks, so all their lives they grew up with quite a bit of confidence and the ability to speak publicly." It was also in her daily interactions with David that she tried to instill maturity in him beyond his years. "I would talk to them like they were adults from the time they were very little." Although religion was central to David's upbringing, Rose didn't impose religion on the children. Instead, she just modeled how positive a force it was in her life. "All the kids knew the church was important to us, but we didn't force them to go on missions or to do anything. They just saw us doing it."

Rose described David as someone who always cared about the larger world around him. Whether it was being the first one to offer to take out the trash or helping a disabled girl at the church, Rose said David was always very "service oriented." "When David was maybe three or four years old, there was this little girl who came to the church and she was in a wheelchair. And when we would get there, David would go straight out to the gate and wait. They would pull up and the dad would take the wheelchair out and get the little girl and David would walk into the church where they were supposed to go."

Music was the prevalent form of entertainment in the Neeleman household. "When we built our house, we put in a speaker system so you could hear music all through the house. We bought all of this classical music so the kids would get it embedded in them." Music also extended to recreational activities. "We loved plays, but musicals even more than plays. When the kids were young, we had quite a nice theater, where traveling musical groups would come through and so we did that a lot."

Rose said that when it came to sports and other extracurricular activities, there were no expectations. "It was like you'd play baseball because it looks fun. . . . When our seventh one took swimming and hated it, it was okay that he quit and then taught himself to swim. I don't think we pushed them at all." At home, Rose always made sure that doing chores was a collaborative activity. "I thought it was important that children work with you, instead of telling them what to do."

David's schooling was a concern for Rose. When David was in the third grade, Rose grew worried about his handwriting and his reading abilities. She later learned that he had a mild learning disability. "I took him one summer to this tutor every day and at the end of the time, the tutor said, 'I think David's mother needs to relax.' And then another teacher, at about the same time, said, 'You shouldn't be worried about David because he's going to have a whole fleet of secretaries to take care of his needs.' "

Heeding the tutor's advice and sensing the truth in the teacher's prophecy, Rose adopted a relaxed attitude toward David's learning disability—an approach that David credits today in the success he's had in overcoming it. "David is the honorary president of Smart Kids, an organization to help kids with learning disabilities, and we were at one of these meetings . . . David was talking about his own ADD. He said, 'You know, people get so anxious and tied up about what college your kids are going to get into.' One of the women asked, 'Were your parents concerned about it?' He said, 'My parents were just very relaxed about it. . . . You know, they were just comfortable with it.' "

Despite Rose's positive attitude, there were moments of adversity when it came to David's learning issues. "When David was three years old, and had just started going to preschool, he ran over to me and put his face down like right above my knees and started to sob because he said, 'I can't sing those hard songs and I can't draw those hard pictures. . . .' The next morning I walked into his room and he was lying there with his hands under his head just staring at the ceiling. . . . I said to David, 'You know, in this life, it's up to you what you want to make of yourself. You can be a big, wonderful man like your dad or you can be a bum on the street. . . . But if you want to be a big, wonderful man like your dad, you're going to have to go to school, you're going to have to go on a mission, you're going to have to do a lot of hard things.' "

Internalizing his mother's "it's up to you" approach, at nineteen David made a life-changing decision. "I was standing in the kitchen, and he came up to me and said, 'I'm ready to go on a mission.' He said, 'Mom, what did you think I'm going to be? A big, wonderful man like dad or a bum?' I was crying, as you can imagine."

Rose said that going on his mission was a pivotal time for David that defined his life and shaped how he runs his business. "David says that he learned that poor people are every bit as happy as rich people, and sometimes more so." On a deeper level, Rose described it as putting him in touch with humanity. "To him, everybody is the same and he treats his employees the same. For instance, all the employees have numbers on their badges, but nobody has a higher number than anybody else."

Rose saw signs of David's interest in aviation at a young age. "When David was young we'd often drive to California, and everybody was crowded in with the wind blowing. David said, 'Wouldn't airline travel be much more enjoyable?' " So while it might not have been his mother's affinity for aviation—she didn't travel on an airline until she was twenty-three—that led David into the business, her parenting style is quite apparent in JetBlue's business model. "David gives his salary to a catastrophic employee fund and the employees match it so if somebody has a disaster or something, there's a special fund. That's very much his personality," a personality that was nurtured by a mother, and a family, steeped in the tradition of helping others.

Suna Oz

Mother of DR. MEHMET OZ

"Don't try to live through them . . . encourage them to persevere
as opposed to enforcing orders."

When Mehmet Oz—widely touted as the most accomplished and respected cardiothoracic surgeon in the United States—started elementary school, his mother, Suna Oz, said she was invited to the school for a special meeting. "His teacher explained to me that Mehmet was fast on his feet and would finish his assignments early and then get restless and naughty." This "restlessness," while grounds for a parent meeting in elementary school, was also the energy that propelled Mehmet to pursue a medical degree at the University of Pennsylvania as well as an MBA at Wharton. He has gone on to perform surgery on some four hundred patients a year, is a professor of cardiac surgery at Columbia University, and director of the Cardiovascular Institute at

Columbian Presbyterian, and directs the Hear Assist Device Program. Mehmet has written more than 350 articles, which have been included in publications ranging from academic journals to magazines such as *Newsweek, Time,* and Oprah's *O. Esquire* magazine singled him out as the best heart surgeon in New York and highlighted his pioneering efforts to combine Western medicine with alternative therapies. Mehmet is married to Lisa Oz and has four children.

Growing up in Istanbul, Suna characterized her own upbringing as more cultural than religious. "I was raised to believe in God, to help others in need, and to set an example of right and wrong. I believe if you look inside yourself, you see the truth." As a young mother at twenty-one, Suna described her marriage to her surgeon husband, Dr. Mustafa Oz, as "happy" and the birth of their first son, Mehmet, as a planned event. Even though Mehmet—the first of three children—did receive a lot of "tender loving care," Suna gave all her children the same attention. Reflecting today on her early child-rearing days, she said, "I felt privileged to nurture my children myself." As might be expected of someone with Mehmet's credentials, Suna said that he started crawling, walking, and talking earlier than she expected. "I just let him develop at his own pace."

When it comes to defining her parenting style, Suna emphasized her desire to cultivate independence and tenacity in her children. "I didn't try to live through them . . . and I gave encouragement to persevere as opposed to enforcing orders." Above all, Suna said that parenting was permeated by her pure, unadulterated love of motherhood. "I really just enjoyed devoting my days to Mehmet. I would choose a book to read to him . . . and then he would read on his own. He was very curious and had a lot of questions to ask." Still, Suna didn't push his development. "I encouraged his activities by being with him, but I never pressured him because I didn't believe in causing a frustrating atmosphere for kids . . . a child should develop at his or her own pace."

The intellectual envrionment in the Oz household was fostered by the strict no television policy. "My husband did not allow our children to watch TV, unless they got permission and then Mehmet would watch *Star Trek*." But Mehmet was hardly a bookworm. Suna recalled, "He played football, basketball, and baseball. Mehmet was actually named first team state in football his senior year of high school." It's this kind of well-roundedness that Suna wanted to instill in her children—from reading to sports to music. "Mehmet and his sisters took piano lessons, which they enjoyed tremendously." Music, though, wasn't just a structured thing in the Oz household. "My husband used to wake up the kids for school early each morning by playing Turkish music extra loudly on the cassette player! That was a real wake-up call!" From the jovial to the serious, Suna said that her marriage was a bedrock of Mehmet's upbringing. "My husband and I had a very stable relationship. We had a real partnership, which was defined by trying to set the right example for our children."

Travel was also a large part of Mehmet's upbringing. With both sets of his grandparents still living in Istanbul, trips abroad were a regular occurrence. "I took the children back to visit Turkey during school breaks and summer vacations, and they loved traveling and being exposed to different cultures." Asked about how this cross-cultural exposure influenced her children, Suna said, "It widened their horizons and taught them different solutions to problems, like how people can learn to survive with very little under difficult conditions as long as they have love and understanding for each other."

Social activity—both with adults and peers—was a staple of Mehmet's childhood. "My husband always had our friends over for dinner, and there were long hours of medical discussions on new developments in science." This, Suna said, rubbed off on Mehmet. "Mehmet was also very sociable and loved to have his friends around the house." When it came to the day-to-day routine, both Suna and her husband stayed involved in the myriad of activities their children were involved in.

Describing her parenting style in more detail, Suna said it was always about the bigger, global picture. "I consider myself a compassionate and supportive teacher of the values that we should all share in life to make the world a peaceful and better place." Distilling it down to its essence, Suna said, "My style of parenting is nurturing and guidance through empathy." She credited Mehmet's success to the distinct roles that she and her husband played in his upbringing. "My husband instilled in Mehmet the same hard work ethic, leadership qualities, and passion for continued learning that he displayed in his own career. I tried to be a compassionate and involved mother balancing the family's emotional life—call it stress management—which I believe showed Mehmet the importance of 'keeping healthy' relationships, especially concerning the priority—family—and inclusive of colleagues and people in general."

Suna and her husband always told Mehmet that they had the highest goals for him. "We were strict in our desire for Mehmet to excel." This, Suna said, was based on what they saw as Mehmet's innate talents and the need to channel them. "We wanted him to get the best grades in the best schools because we felt early on that Mehmet was gifted with a beautiful mind and needed guidance and encouragement to get the best out of him." But it also came down to the little things, Suna recalled. "My husband made an effort to take Mehmet along with him when he made rounds at the hospital on Saturday mornings. He wanted our son to be a surgeon and familiarized him with the field early on to spark interest." Suna's advice to mothers today is timeless and simple: "Just love, care, and be a part of your child's life and always keep a warm hand on their shoulder."

Beverly Anne Patrick

Mother of DANICA PATRICK

"You get out what you put in."

*B*everly Ann Patrick—the mother of racing phenomenon Danica Patrick—said that as a child Danica did not gravitate toward toy cars. Today, however, Danica has forged a wildly successful career around cars. Danica began her racing career in the early 1990s when she won several national championships in go-karting. After a decade of successfully competing in a male-dominated sport, Danica became the fourth woman to race in the Indianapolis 500 in 2005. She also became the first female driver to lead nineteen laps at the Indianapolis 500. In 2005, Danica finished twelfth in the IRL IndyCar Series Championship and moved up three spots to finish ninth in 2006.

Danica was named Rookie of the Year in the 2005 IRL Championship, becoming the first IndyCar driver to be featured on the cover of *Sports Illustrated* in twenty years. She was nominated for Best Breakthrough Athlete for the 2005 ESPY Awards and was named the Sportsman of the Year by the Woman's Sports Foundation. Danica was also designated the 2006 Female Athlete of the Year by the United States Sports Academy. She has been featured in *TV Guide* and *ESPN the Magazine* as well as on *Jimmy Kimmel Live!*, *Today*, *The Late Show with David Letterman*, and *The Tony Danza Show*. She has hosted several TV shows on Spike TV and was featured in the 2005 documentary *Girl Racers*, as well as appearing in Secret deodorant commercials. In May 2006, she published her autobiography, *Danica: Crossing the Line*. Danica lives in Arizona with her husband, Paul Hospenthal.

Beverly described an informal atmosphere to Danica's upbringing, but one that was filled with all the staples of a happy, enriched childhood. "I read to her, I played with her, and I put on music," Beverly recalled. Instead of scheduling activities, she just encouraged Danica to go outside and play. "I would go out and do yard work and have Danica and her sister, Brooke, playing out in the yard, and we had a garden, so they would entertain themselves with things out there. There certainly wasn't always scheduled playtime." Sports, on the other hand, were slightly more scheduled. "They took tumbling and dance classes. . . . When she [Danica] was seven, she did T-ball, and then in high school she did cheerleading as well."

Social activity, Beverly said, revolved around the family. "I would say we were not overly social because we were a single-income family, and we spent more time at home than going out," a fact that Beverly anything but begrudges. "Family was just very important. We had all different generations of our family around. Danica's father's grandfather was a staple in her life. He was always around. So I would say that for us being social was more about being with family than with outsiders. We were pretty much home people."

As such, spending time as a family was the cornerstone of Danica's childhood. "We were always, always together," Beverly said.

"That was probably one of the craziest things . . . everything we did we did together." In fact, it was a family outing that exposed Danica to go-kart racing. "My husband had been working seven days a week and we decided that we needed to have something fun to do as a family one day a week. It was actually Brooke's idea to start go-karting. She was the one who wanted to go first, and Danica was a little reluctant, but she said she'd try it. But as soon as we got started with go-karting, Danica just became so driven and so passionate about wanting to do it all the time. I mean, she wanted us to go in the middle of the week. They had open practice, and she could never get enough of it. We never had to force her to go. . . . Danica has just been really lucky that she found her passion at thirteen."

Although at times it was difficult to watch her daughter participate in such a dangerous sport, Beverly believed so strongly in Danica's passion that she supported it wholeheartedly. It was this flexible, take-it-as-it-comes attitude that Beverly said she tried to maintain. "When she went to England at sixteen to take her go-kart racing to the next level, we really wanted her to stay in school, but she decided not to. . . . I told her if she went over there and it didn't work out then she could come back and go to college." Still, even though Beverly knew it was the right thing to do to encourage Danica to go, she said, "I don't think I ever hung up the phone without crying when she was over there. It was tough." Reflecting more on how she handled that period, Beverly said, "It sounds kind of corny, but for Danica to have gotten that far and then to say to her, 'It's too dangerous,' just didn't seem like the right thing to do. Also, we trusted that she would be safe and smart in her choices. More importantly, it just seemed like her destiny to be doing this."

This is something that Beverly certainly intuited correctly. "Danica became so serious about racing. I mean, she was breaking track records probably five months into racing go-karts. She really liked the feeling of winning, but she didn't jump up and down and say, 'Look at me, I won.' She just projected the confidence that she knew this was what she was supposed to be doing." Even with all of Danica's success, Beverly said she was not a pushy, sideline parent. "My husband and I always told her she could quit at any point, and we meant that."

Beverly didn't have specific expectations for Danica. "I just always wanted her to do the best she could. I never had any preconceived expectation of what grade point average she should get. As long as I felt that she was doing the best she could, I felt that was fine." It was also Beverly's belief that people progress better with praise and encouragement than they do with criticism—an approach she brought to parenting even when things went awry. "I remember once Danica forgot where she was in the middle of a dance recital and started crying. . . . Afterward I consoled her and told her that it was fine. . . . I just always let her know, no matter what, that she was doing a good job."

The foundation of their family, Beverly said, has been her twenty-six-year marriage to her husband, TJ. "As parents we were really supportive of each other, but we took on different roles. I took the lead when they were young, and when they were teenagers they needed to have stricter rules and their dad took charge of the rules." However, it wasn't only TJ who was the arbiter of the rules in the Patrick household. "I made sure that wherever she went—whether it was to a friend's house, a movie, or whatever—that I knew where she was going and who she was going with. At the time, I remember Danica saying to us, 'You are the strictest parents ever.'" Resolute in her belief that children need limits, Beverly always told her, "Well, that's just the way it is." Although going to church wasn't a weekly ritual in the Patrick family, religion colored how Beverly imparted morals and values to Danica. "We tried to teach them right and wrong and good and bad, rooting as much of it as possible in religion."

Ruminating on Danica's success, Beverly said she tried to instill a certain resiliency in her daughter. "It's tough out there. It's like playing the lottery. You have good days and bad days, and there are more bad days than good days. So it's real easy to give up in any sport, and England was extremely tough. It was very lonely and she didn't have a very good support team, but she learned a lot." Beverly said it was always extremely important to her that Danica experience that feeling of accomplishment on her own—that no one pushed her to do it. "I think because we were sort of hands-off, she's very self-motivated. She pushed herself hard enough and at a pretty young age."

Asked about any special phrases or words of encouragement she remembered giving Danica, Beverly said, "I used to tell her, 'You get out what you put in,'" something that Beverly made sure to model in her own life. "I always had a strong work ethic. When Danica and Brooke were little we had our glass shop, so they'd be with the babysitter during the day. I'd go home at five o'clock and my husband and I would go back to work until midnight, and they saw us do that every day. We really operationalized the saying of, 'You get out what you put in.'"

Beverly's advice for mothers today: "I think kids need to have people asking them what they are doing and where they are going. They have to answer for somebody." As for Beverly's other words of wisdom to her daughter, "Always be a lady"—advice that Danica has certainly put her own spin on!

Susan Poster

Mother of MERYL POSTER

"Be firm, but do not break their spirit."

Susan Poster—the mother of former Miramax executive Meryl Poster—said that ever since her daughter was a little girl, Meryl expressed a desire to be famous. "As she grew older, she said she wanted to be famous like Barbara Walters." Although she's taken on a more behind-the-scenes approach, today Meryl is a famous name within the movie industry. She worked at Miramax for sixteen years, starting as an executive assistant to the copresident of production. During her tenure at Miramax, Meryl executive-produced films, including *Chicago, The Cider House Rules, Chocolat,* and *Cop Land.* As a studio executive, she oversaw *Finding Neverland, Good Will Hunting,* and *Shakespeare in Love,* among many others. All of this led to the offer she received in 2005 from NBC to come on board to produce both TV shows and feature projects. Meryl is married to television commercial director Daniel Levinson and has two children.

Susan described her own upbringing as one that was infused with love, warmth, and a lot of quality family time. "My grandparents—Meryl's great-grandparents—lived down the street from us. . . . I was raised by two loving parents and enjoyed a wonderful relationship with both of them." Growing up in a middle-class family, Susan said, influenced how she raised Meryl and her older brother. "I came from a middle-class family that enabled us to enjoy 'the good things in life.' I wanted my children to have those benefits. And, fortunately, my husband and I were financially able to give our children even more than I received."

Replicating her experience in a tight-knit family, Susan made home life one of the centerpieces of Meryl's upbringing, whether it was through informal activities or through religious traditions. "My parents would come to visit every Sunday. . . . On Friday nights we used to have dinner together as a family. . . . We weren't very religious people, but we enjoyed the culture of Judaism, we lit candles on Friday night, and taught them the importance of giving charity. . . . We spent weekends together going to the theater, visiting friends or relatives, and we took the kids on weekend trips to Amish country and Washington, D.C." Susan also credited her forty-six-year marriage to her husband as providing the linchpin for their strength. Reflecting today, she said, "We were a stable family unit due to the fact that we had high morals, and we had fun together."

As might be expected from a movie studio executive, Susan said that Meryl excelled verbally at a young age—and hit all of the developmental milestones ahead of schedule. "Meryl crawled at ten months, walked at a year, and talked at fifteen months, and hasn't stopped since!" Susan emphasized, however, that she and her husband were always intent on letting these milestones happen in their own time. Still, Susan always read to Meryl. In addition to exposing

Meryl to Dr. Seuss and all the classic children's books, she would impart her personal history through books. "I wanted Meryl to learn about our family and their experiences in the Russian Revolution, the Depression, and World War II." When it came to the lighter stuff, Susan taught Meryl the entire album of *Color Me Barbra* when she was four years old. "Meryl always enjoyed singing and dancing, and I always took her to musical theater and movies." And to round it all out, "Meryl also took ballet lessons, played tennis and baseball, and swam," Susan said.

Susan, though, was hardly an aggressive mother. Although she had high expectations for both Meryl and her brother, she never pushed for that A or B. "I just told them to do the best they could and gave them praise and encouragement." Susan described her parenting style as a cocktail. "I was authoritative, nurturing, understanding, and strict when I needed to be, but I was always loving and affectionate." However, Susan said that she was the stronger parental figure and wasn't timid about outlining the rules, if that was what the situation called for. "When I said 'no,' I stuck to what I said, at least most of the time."

According to Susan, Meryl had a strong personality growing up and often wanted things "her way." Instead of trying to fight against this trait, Susan said she actually made a concerted effort not to squelch Meryl's spark. "Meryl was a very outspoken toddler and young child. When she was in first, second, and third grade, her teacher called me to school to tell me that Meryl was slightly disruptive and often talked out of turn. I told the teacher to be firm with her, but not to break her spirit. . . . She possessed something special that I didn't want to lose." In another example of Meryl's fiercely independent streak, Susan recalled that in nursery school all the children were making pictures for Father's Day, and Meryl wanted to make a pair of house slippers instead. "So I helped her take a shoe from the house, trace it, and we glued it together."

From helping Meryl with school projects, to becoming the

president of the PTA, Susan was very involved in every aspect of her children's school life. "I was the class mother, I went on field trips. . . . When Meryl was in high school, I volunteered in the library one day a week and at lunchtime I took her friends to Burger King. They still talk about it to this day!"

When asked what advice she has for other mothers, Susan said it's about letting children have as many experiences as possible. "I exposed Meryl to a wide variety of activities. . . . One summer she went to a special tennis camp in Canada, one summer she attended a ski school in the Alps, and she studied abroad in college. If my husband and I were a little apprehensive, Meryl would assure us that the benefits outweighed any risk. I think that all of those experiences helped her to become a strong, independent woman." As well as exposing Meryl to an assortment of experiences, Susan sought and cultivated her own passions. "I was interested in the activities that I shared with the children. I also would take a class each semester: art appreciation, Italian lessons, business classes, and music appreciation."

Susan certainly didn't give specific direction to Meryl when it came to choosing a career. Rather, she said her encouragement was just about helping Meryl with whatever project she was working on at the time. She also gave her some sage advice that has certainly served her well: "I told her it is better to give than receive; if you don't have anything nice to say, don't say it at all; when you play with a group of children, don't exclude anyone; and you will always find someone who is prettier or has more than you, so be happy with what you have and who you are."

Asked about what defines her as a parent, Susan said it's captured by something her son said to her, "Mom, you are the most reliable person in the world."

Marcia Ratner

Mother of BRETT RATNER

"Even if they fail, tell him to keep trying. Look the beast in the eye, and keep on trucking."

arcia Ratner, the mother of one of Hollywood's most successful directors—Brett Ratner—said she used to come to school and embarrass him with all of her kvelling. "I used to come to school and say, 'Look at my gorgeous boy. He is so beautiful.' I would praise everything he did." Decades later, Marcia said, the praising hasn't stopped—and for good reason: Brett's seven feature films have grossed over one billion dollars worldwide. At twenty-six years old, he directed his first feature film, the surprise box office hit *Money Talks*. He followed that success with the romantic fantasy drama *The Family Man*. Brett made his first foray into the world of suspense thrillers with his fifth feature film, *Red Dragon*, the *Silence of the Lambs* prequel. He shattered several box office records with the release of *X-Men* and directed the third installment of the blockbuster *Rush Hour* franchise in 2007. When he isn't making box office history, Brett devotes his time to the Chrysalis Foundation, which helps economically disadvantaged and homeless individuals change their lives through jobs. For his work with the organization, Brett was the recipient of the Spirit of the Chrysalis Award.

Marcia, who was born in Havana, Cuba, described a fascination with all things Latin growing up. "There was always this vivacious feeling in our house . . . we always had all this dancing." Although Marcia was raised in a "nuclear" family, by parents who were married for fifty-five years, she said her parenting approach was to do everything *opposite* from her parents. When applied, this meant that Brett had a lot more rope and freedom than Marcia did. "Whatever he wanted to do, I let him do. If he wanted to make a comic book at eleven o'clock at night, I'd say that's a great idea and I'd stay up to help him. They were more traditional. I was more out of the box."

Marcia emphasized, too, how much she went to bat for Brett. "One day Brett's teacher called me into school and said that Brett was clowning around, disrupting the whole class. The teacher told me, 'Your child has a discipline problem, and I'm going to fail him.' I fought for him, and what happened was that he didn't get transferred out of the class. Instead, he stuck it out and got a B." While it was a small event in the scheme of things, "It was a defining moment for Brett because he felt very supported."

"Engagement," Marcia said, was critical to Brett's upbringing. "I would always encourage him to ask a lot of questions by asking *him* questions. 'Brett, what do you think about the tree? How do you feel about this or that? Do you like that person? Why? What did you like about them?'" But it was more than just engaging Brett that Marcia described; she put him in situations where he had to engage with other people and the world. "When he was eight or nine, we started traveling around the world. We would sleep on the trains. I just love people, so I wanted Brett to have the exposure. . . . A lot of times when we were traveling, we'd have an entourage by the end of the day." It was all part of Marcia's belief that the more you give, the more you get.

To put it simply, Marcia said, "I found excitement in everything that I did. I think that rubbed off on him." As such, Marcia described how she was able to take "normal" activities, such as reading, to the next level. "I would read to him, but they turned out to be more like discussions. I would read something and then we would discuss it." While Marcia had a lot of openness about the way she approached the world, she was strict about certain things, such as television. "To this day, there is no TV in my house. I just hated the noise. I think I instilled in Brett that you have to develop your own resources and that is how you expand your own energy—not by having outside stimulation."

To encourage Brett to tap into his talents and interests, Marcia didn't put pressure on him to succeed. "I just encouraged his thoughts, and I just let him do anything and everything, even if I thought it was wrong." As opposed to wanting to shelter Brett from the world and the repercussions of his actions, Marcia used them as a teaching tool. "I remember once we were in the Dominican Republic, and Brett wanted to rent a golf cart. I didn't think it was such a good idea. The golf cart ended up flipping over and his finger was sliced off. We had to take a three-hour drive to a doctor. He learned his lesson right away. I let him pay for his own mistakes." Marcia credited this approach for Brett's lucid thought process today. "I think that understanding the repercussions of his actions made him really focused and involved. He became totally present and was able to think through things, like movie projects. He's able to look at the whole picture."

It was Brett's ability to be "present" that Marcia said she focused on and gave her the window into Brett's enormous potential. "Even when he was two years old he was different from everyone else. He was totally present. He was curious. He asked a lot of questions. He had a lot of charisma. He had that twinkle in his eye."

Marcia's bigger-picture parenting goals were about trying to instill confidence and, as a corollary, self-reliance. "I remember when I would tell my parents that I wanted to go to camp with friends they would say, 'What if you miss us in the middle of the night?' They always looked at the bad side of things. When Brett went to camp he said to me, 'What if I miss you?' I said, 'You can write to me, or I can come get you on visiting day.' I gave him so many alternatives."

Marcia said that she was the "hub" while Brett was growing up. "Since Brett was the only child, all the kids would come to my house. . . . If he played football, I was there. I was the hub." Above all, her parenting was defined by immersing Brett in the world—a value that trumped almost everything. "If there was something more important, like a museum opening or a concert, I would take him out of school. I thought that was equally as important. I engaged him in real life."

Marcia reflected on the resiliency she imparted to Brett: "Even if he failed, I would tell him to keep trying. I said to him, 'Look the beast in the eye, and keep on trucking.' I would say that a lot. I can protect myself from the sharks. I gave Brett that edge." Condensing such a sweeping, grandiose parenting style down to a sentence, Marcia said, "I just didn't shield him from any sorrow . . . and I also tried to cultivate generosity because that is how you become open to the world."

Emma Reid

Mother of ANTONIO "L.A." REID

"Parenting is always about two things: letting children be
themselves and not forcing your dreams on them."

Emma Reid, mother of Antonio "L.A." Reid, the chairman of
Island Def Jam Music Group, said that when Antonio was
growing up there was always music playing. "We just loved
it," Emma said. Antonio has taken his childhood passion for music
and parlayed it to become one of the most successful executives in
the music industry. Antonio is going into his third year as chairman of one of the largest record labels in the country. He has helped
shape the careers of some of the most notable people in the music
industry. Mariah Carey, Kanye West, Jay-Z, and Bon Jovi are among
many artists he has helped go platinum. Antonio is hardly a stranger
to the performance side of the business. He is an accomplished
drummer, songwriter, and producer, drawing influence from

musicians such as Miles Davis, Sly Stone, the Beatles, and Led Zeppelin. In addition to all of his professional accomplishments, Antonio is active in PENCIL (Public Education Needs Civic Involvement in Learning), an organization that promotes civic involvement in New York City public schools. Antonio is married with children.

Antonio was the third of four children, but Emma said that birth order did not impact the attention she gave to any of her children. "I just kind of spread it around," she said, reflecting on those early years. Harkening back to a time when there wasn't such a thing as family planning, Emma said that Antonio was a surprise. "We didn't plan pregnancies back then."

Raising her four children as a single mother (Emma and her husband divorced when Antonio was two) and coming from a low-income family herself, Emma said that life was all about trade-offs. "When you sacrifice so much, you also miss out on so much, so you want to make sure you can give your kids the best of everything." For Emma, "giving Antonio the best" meant making sure he pursued his dreams.

When Antonio was five, Emma noticed that he would stand around and beat on something long enough until he got a rhythm. As part of her parenting philosophy of helping her son build his interests, Emma bought him a set of drums. In addition, she encouraged his musical endeavors by just showing up to his performances. "I would always tell him how proud I was of what he was doing when I went to his concerts. At fifteen, Antonio was already playing in concerts in the park!" Antonio's musical talent didn't end with the drums; Emma recalled that he was a gifted piano player as well, a talent that didn't take buying a piano to develop. "We didn't have a piano at home. He would just play at school, or wherever we'd go, he'd find a piano and play on it."

Describing how Antonio developed at his own pace, Emma said that she didn't push certain developmental milestones. "We certainly didn't have a set time where we read every day." What was an everyday staple, however, was music. "There was always music play-ing, whether we were at home or in the car. . . . We listened to it all: jazz, rock 'n' roll, and rhythm and blues, but it was a lot of jazz." The informal, spontaneous moments, where they would just sit on the floor and play, were what Emma said captured the spirit of Anto-nio's upbringing. "We'd play a lot of board games, and just sit on the floor and talk together." Although Emma said her biggest regret is that she wished she could have spent more time with Antonio, she found ways to integrate her work and quality time with her chil-dren. "I did a lot of sewing at home—I was making draperies—and Antonio would always help me with that, and then he would go with me to hang them at people's homes."

As informal as things could be, however, Emma said she was definitely a "no-nonsense" type of mother. "I didn't like him hang-ing out on the street. As kids, they just want to stand on street cor-ners with other kids. I didn't allow that." Asked how she was able to command such a presence with her kids in their rebellious teenage years, Emma said, "I guess I just had a certain look on my face. . . . My kids were so funny. They would look at me and say, 'Don't mess with that lady.' So when I told them something, they basically would follow my instructions." Looking at it in the bigger picture, Emma reflected that being a no-nonsense mother was how she kept it all intact. "My children knew that I meant what I said and that's how we were able to remain a stable unit."

Raising Antonio and his three siblings as a working mother had an enormous effect on how Emma approached parenting. "I really prioritized spending the weekends with them because I didn't get to see them as much during the week. We would all go to church on Sundays." But Antonio, like so many children, resisted this Sunday ritual. "At an early age Antonio let me know that he didn't like reli-gion." Emma's style, however, was not to push it on him. "Even if he didn't want to go to church, I would not let that spoil my day. I'd say, 'You stay here and I'm going to go.' I'd let him make his own decisions, because you can't force religion on children." Even as a single mother raising four children, Emma found time for herself. "After church on Sundays, I would come and play poker with a group of ladies. The kids loved it because they were able to spend time doing what they wanted to do in the house." Growing up in what Emma described as a "very regimented" household, Sunday afternoon provided a break from the strict routine of homework, dinner, and bedtime. Juggling a job, children, and a household, Emma said that though she was in contact with the children's teachers, attending *all* the PTA meetings and school events was not realistic. "I didn't attend too many of them because of my work schedule."

Still, Emma was involved in Antonio's school life. "I definitely pushed him to do well in school." Rewarding good, hard work was also part of the parenting strategy. "My children would get a quarter for every 'A' on their report card. It really got them excited and motivated them." When it came to encouraging Antonio toward his bigger dreams and goals, Emma told him to "dream big" and that he could be anything he wanted to be if he put his heart and mind to it. But even as a mother who bought him his first set of drums and attended all his summer concerts in the park, Emma didn't have any idea that he was going to be as big a success as he is today. "I guess my defining moment was when he was fourteen and I saw him play at a concert here in Cincinnati. That's when it really clicked for me. I saw him get up there and speak to this large audience. I was so proud of him." Emma said her parenting was always about two things: letting her children be themselves, and not forcing *her* dreams on them—a method that certainly helped Antonio pursue *his* dreams.

Bette Sacco

Mother of AMY SACCO

"Don't push children into things they are not really interested in."

*B*ette Sacco—the mother of Amy Sacco, a New York nightclub owner and restaurateur—said that as a child Amy never liked to go to bed. "Amy was always a night owl. In fact, she was such a night owl that I had a hard time getting her up to go to morning kindergarten. I had to put her in the afternoon session because she functioned so poorly in the morning. Her biological clock just wasn't set that way." Amy has gone on to turn her nocturnal side into a booming career. She is often referred to as "the queen of New York nightlife" and is credited with converting New York City's Chelsea into the go-to party destination with hot spots such as Lot 61 and Bungalow 8. Bungalow 8 is frequented by such celebrities as Demi Moore, Ashton Kutcher, Naomi Watts, and the Hilton sisters and was featured on HBO's *Sex and the City*. Amy is also the owner of the restaurant Bette, named after her mother. Amy's film credits include *Kettle of Fish* and *The Doorman*. The *Daily News* named her one of the "100 Women Who Shape Our City." Amy was recently signed by Creative Artists Agency to do a scripted adaptation of her life, which will be produced by another New York City icon, Sarah Jessica Parker. In addition, Amy is taking her empire across the Atlantic. Bugalow 8 opened in London in September 2007 in the St. Martins Land Hotel. Her book *Cocktails* was published in 2006. Amy is also involved in Free Arts NYC, a nonprofit organization dedicated to bringing the arts into the lives of abused, neglected, and at-risk children and their families, as well as another New York–based arts organization, The Art Production Fund.

Amy's strong work ethic is a direct result of her mother's influence—Bette started working for her father, Amy's grandfather, when she was eight years old. "I think my background gave me very strong guidelines for work and high moral standards. My mom really insisted on that." Although Bette was raised in what she described as a "poor" household, there was no limit to the things she thought she could achieve. "My mother, Amy's grandmother, used to tell me, 'Just because we are poor doesn't mean that you aren't going to grow up as a lady. . . .' Overall, she just did everything with grace and dignity, which set a great example for me."

Amy, the last of eight children, had a live-in team of teachers. Even with such a large family, the Saccos ate dinner together every night. However, family time extended beyond just dinner. Bette said, "I had the grandparents over almost every week. We had a big Sunday dinner and I think the values and the habits you set up within the family have a really lasting effect on children." Sacco family dinners weren't about eating and running. Bette said they took Sunday dinners as an opportunity to discuss things. "I think just being together as a family was so important."

As the youngest of eight, Amy certainly had an unusual position in the family, and the benefit of having a mother who had experienced each phase she went through seven times before. "I think my experience having the other children helped a great deal when I was raising Amy. I learned the important parenting lesson of 'Don't push children into things they are not really interested in.'" Bette said that, as might be expected from a youngest child, Amy always wished she were older than her age. "When she was twelve she wanted to be sixteen. When she was sixteen she couldn't wait to be twenty-one." And while for some girls the desire to be older was about being able to wear makeup and go on dates, Bette said Amy wanted to be older so she could get a job. "She always wanted to go to work. That's all she ever thought about."

Although Amy was too young to go to work, Bette realized that her daughter needed to participate in some type of activity that simulated a work experience. "I said, you have to try Brownies, and she didn't mind that because some of her friends were there. And I think that's when I realized that she had a lot of leadership and business ability, because she sold three hundred boxes of Girl Scout cookies all by herself." According to Bette, Amy was a precocious child, and when she was five years old she would put her hand out and say, in a deep husky voice, "Hi, I'm Amy and I'm incorrigible."

When it came to encouraging her daughter, Bette supported Amy in anything she was enthusiastic about. "She always said that she wanted to be somebody and go someplace. Amy told me, 'I'm not going stay in this small town. I'm going to go somewhere and I'm going to be somebody.' And I probably just merely said to her at the time, 'That's right. You go for it.'" Above all, motherhood was a complete labor of love for Bette. "I was very, very happy being a mother. I was absolutely delighted. I wouldn't have ever wanted to do anything else."

Bette said she always perceived a certain warmth about Amy—the warmth that would help endear New York City nightlife to her. "Amy is by nature a very affectionate type of person, a very loving person. . . . I think her warmth brought people to her. I really welcomed her warmth and tried to cultivate it." Not only did Bette encourage Amy's warmth, she let it have a positive influence on her. "Amy really taught me how to be more affectionate. . . . She made me sit down once in a while and she'd wrap her arms and legs around me and hug me." Bette said she met Amy where she was at. "I realized she just needed more affection than some other children, so I became more affectionate."

It was this approach of not trying to squelch, or change, Amy's personality that Bette said defined her parenting style. "I remember her first-grade teacher called me and said, 'Mrs. Sacco, I love your daughter, but you must tell her that she cannot teach the class.' I had a talk with Amy, but at the same time I didn't want to mute her 'take charge' personality."

Letting her daughter develop at her pace, without pressure, was how Bette parented throughout Amy's childhood. "I always told her to pursue her dreams. I stood behind her all the way." Even when Amy wanted to do things slightly ahead of the curve, Bette was supportive. "I probably wouldn't have encouraged her to get a job at thirteen, but that's what she did. She came home and told me she got a job. I said, 'Honey you're not old enough to work. You don't have working papers.' She said, 'No, but I look old enough so they didn't ask me.' That's how she got her first job at a restaurant."

Reflecting on what helped Amy achieve all that she has, Bette recalled the old adage of the apple not falling far from the tree. "I think it has something to do with my dad because he was in the restaurant business, and I was trained in that business. So I think she saw me in the kitchen so much and that was something that she just naturally gravitated to." However, Bette said she didn't pressure Amy into that career path. "I always said to her, 'You're free to choose whatever path you wish, but I just want you to be the best you can be in that career.'" In addition, Bette recalled specific sayings she used to encourage Amy. "I would tell her, 'Some things, like choices, have consequences. This, too, shall pass—if they were having a hard time or if something really went wrong. Poverty builds character. Bloom where you are planted.' " Bette also emphasized her fervor for motherhood. "I had a passion for motherhood, which enabled me to give my best to my children."

As for Bette's take on her role in helping instill the success principle in her entrepreneurial daughter—it was all about *active* listening. "I think you really just have to be a good listener. You have to try to hear what they're feeling and try to pick up on the direction that the child wants to go." Crediting a combination of nurture and nature, Bette said, too, "It's Amy's sense of humor that got her where she is today."

Jean Hayes

Mother of DIANE SAWYER

"I just tried awfully hard to do what was best for them,
yet to be kind."

*D*iane Sawyer said she never understood how her mother—
Jean Hayes—did it. When speaking to her mother, Diane
said, "I mean to teach school, take us to lessons, cook dinner, clean house, and start the church in the neighborhood . . . I
still don't know when you slept, Mom." The irony is that people
wonder the same thing about Diane. She anchors ABC's *Good Morning America* five days a weeks as well as *Primetime,* not to mention her
frequent appearances on other news programs. Working her way up
from a local reporter in Kentucky to Nixon's press team to the *CBS
Morning News,* Diane eventually landed a job as coanchor of *60 Minutes.* In 1989, she moved to ABC to coanchor *Primetime Live* with Sam
Donaldson, and in 1999, she was named anchor for *Good Morning*

America. During her three decades in the news business, Diane has received numerous Emmy Awards, Peabody Awards, and the Robert F. Kennedy Journalism Award. She has also been inducted into the Broadcast Magazine Hall of Fame and the Television Academy of Fame. Sawyer has been married to film and theatrical director Mike Nichols since 1988.

Displaying the signs of being an überachiever since infancy, Diane hit all the milestones—walking, talking, and crawling—early. Although Diane would go on to be an icon of television news, Jean said their family didn't have a TV until Diane was five or six. Jean described herself as an involved parent. "When Diane wanted to do theater, I would go in the afternoon after school and take her down. I was very involved in whatever she was doing." As part of that approach, Jean signed her children up for a lot of lessons. "They had tap and ballet lessons, and lots of physical workouts." She was motivated, in part, by her desire for her daughter to have more opportunities than she did. "I would have liked to play the piano, but we didn't have a piano at the time."

Reflecting on her childhood, Diane said that one of the most important things her mother instilled in her was the importance of finishing what she started—a value Diane has certainly manifested in her career. "My mother always made it clear, 'If you do it, commit to it, and do it as nearly perfectly as you can.'" Diane said this mentality definitely trickled down to her. "I think if it's worth doing, it's worth doing right." Jean put it more holistically when she said, "I just tried awfully hard to do what was best for them, yet to be kind."

Recalling how committed Jean was to her children, Diane said, "I don't remember a day that my mother didn't get up early, put on her perfect makeup with her perfectly combed hair, and set about the day. It was never just, 'This is the day for me to be a slob. Leave me alone.' It was never one of those." Jean said that even though she was always perfectly groomed, she didn't have expectations for her daughter to be perfect. For Jean, it was just about having Diane do things she liked, and for her to do it as well as she could. "It didn't have to be perfect. I just wanted her to succeed."

A tight-knit, cohesive family was the core of Diane's upbringing. Married to her husband for thirty years, Jean said they would always try to eat dinner as a family. She emphasized, too, her desire as a parent to have things work out for Diane, an effort that has certainly seen its dividends. "You know, we really wanted everything to go well, and we worked at trying to make things go well and to help them."

Imparting a sense of curiosity—a quality every journalist requires—is what Diane said stands out about her mother's gifts. "The main thing was that my mother was so curious about the world. Her curiosity was part of our DNA. . . . She still watches the news all the time and she's traveled so much and when she does, if there is a statue to be seen, she's going to see it. She is going to see everything in the book, so there's just this great hunger to know about the world, and that was implicit in every part of our lives. . . . Her interests really sparked our interests."

Jean said she was also careful to always listen to Diane when she spoke about her dreams and aspirations, making sure to always express the deep faith she had in Diane's abilities. "I just always felt that she could accomplish what she wanted to accomplish if she really put her heart into it. And she did." Always having open channels of communications, Jean said, helped further Diane's dreams and goals. "Diane would tell me what she wanted to do, and I was behind her, whatever she wanted to do. . . . I just wanted her to be the best that she could be and be happy with what she was doing."

Instilling a sense of resiliency, an essential quality for someone working in an industry as publicly scrutinized as television, in Diane was also important to Jean. "If something didn't work out, I'd say, 'Try again' . . . but basically she always succeeded." Her other philosophy about success, which she imparted to Diane, was: "If you keep *trying* to succeed, you finally reach success." Reflecting on how she helped Diane get where she is today, Jean said that "she really cared deeply about Diane doing the things that she wanted to do to be able to succeed. Anything I could do to help her succeed, I did." Although Jean made no secret of how proud she is of Diane today, she said she tempered the accolades, instilling in Diane a sense of humility that is rare for someone of her stature. "We were both so proud of Diane, but yet we tried to be limited in our expressions. I just don't like going around bragging."

Arline Schwarzman

Mother of STEPHEN SCHWARZMAN

"I brought him up the way I was raised—
with love and happiness."

*A*rline Schwarzman, the mother of Stephen Schwarzman—
chairman, CEO, and cofounder of the Blackstone Group, one
of the leading and most profitable private equity firms in the
country—said, when talking about her son's myriad of accomplishments, "You've come a long way, baby." This phrase has a particular
resonance spoken by a mother whose son was touted in the February
2007 issue of *Fortune* as "Wall Street's man of the moment." Arline's
assessment of "You've come a long way, baby" only begins to capture
the many incredible milestones of Stephen's life—both professional
and personal. At the age of thirty-one, Stephen became a managing

director at Lehman Brothers. He then went on to serve as chairman of the firm's mergers and acquisitions committee.

In addition to his illustrious finance career, Stephen is the chairman of the board of the John F. Kennedy Center for the Performing Arts. He is a member of the Council on Foreign Relations; on the boards of the New York Public Library, the New York City Ballet, and the Film Society of Lincoln Center; and is also a trustee of the Frick Collection in New York City. But perhaps most telling of his success is Stephen's resounding "yes" to the question, "Are you happy?" "I recently asked him that," Arline said. "He gave an unequivocal yes. He said, 'I have a terrific wife, who is my lover and best friend. I have incredible children. I have risen to the top of my career. I have activities I love to do, and I'm fortunate to have the means to give *tzedak*—charity.' "

Being her firstborn child, Arline said, put Stephen in a unique, often lauded, position in the family. "When he stood up, we applauded. When he drank from a cup, it was a big deal. When he learned to tie his shoes, we marveled." However, with each ensuing child, Arline said she modulated her praise and marveling. "If the second or third child went to school without knowing how to tie their shoes, it wasn't a big deal." Stephen, though, certainly didn't buckle under that pressure. In fact, he thrived. "Stephen was always a busy and motivated child, a good student, and very popular," Arline said, recalling his childhood accomplishments. "He was class president and student council president. Stephen had a fire in his belly and his own agenda."

Growing up, the Schwarzmans did not have the kind of wealth that Stephen has today. Arline described Stephen's upbringing as "middle class." When asked what the most potent force was that influenced how she raised Stephen, Arline cited the model of her upbringing: "I brought him up the way I was raised—with love and happiness."

Arline's vision was to have extraordinary children. "My mother always said to me that I could have been a successful CEO, like Stephen, but my focus was on my children." Reflecting on how she cultivated Stephen to be so ambitious, Arline said it was by example, citing her litany of accomplishments. "I was the kind of person who was president of the school, outstanding camper, and I was always on the forefront. I loved competition. And I expected the same of my son." To groom Stephen for greatness, Arline took a buffet approach, giving him a bit of everything to sample. "I exposed him to horseback riding, tennis, the Boy Scouts, and I always had my eyes on the Ivy League for him." Having a multitude of interests was something that Arline modeled in her own life as well. "My husband and I were lifelong members of the Philadelphia Orchestra, we always went to the Philadelphia Museum, and I collected art as well." Even in her "empty nest" stage, Arline has continued to feed her interests. "I told my husband that after the kids left, there were three things I wanted to do. I wanted to travel the world, which I've done. I wanted to learn to water ski, and I wanted a boat." Needless to say, Arline has fulfilled this ambitious triad of goals.

Amid all of Stephen's extracurricular activities, Arline said she didn't have much time to be strict about television. "I wasn't particular about what he watched and the length of time he watched." The most organic of Stephen's pastimes was neighborhood playtime. Befuddled at the idea that a parent would initiate playdates, Arline said, "Oh, he just went out the back door. There were millions of kids." Like most children, Stephen had that one activity—Hebrew school—he railed against. "I remember he ran away one day. I had to go to the playground and drag him back." Still, even with his less than enthusiastic attitude about Hebrew school, Arline said religion was a very important part of Stephen's life growing up. "We'd have Shabbat dinner on Friday and go to temple on Saturday."

Describing her marriage, Arline likened it to the prototypical TV family: *Ozzie and Harriet*. Putting her own spin on it, Arline described her marriage as a genuine partnership. "My husband and I

Marion Scotto

Mother of ROSANNA, ELAINA, ANTHONY JR., AND JOHN SCOTTO

by Scotto

"I always told my children I was their mother, not their friend, which meant that I gave them strategic direction."

Marion Scotto, the matriarch of the landmark New York restaurant Fresco by Scotto and mother to the quartet of restaurateurs—Rosanna, Elaina, John, and Anthony Jr.—said she was raised to work hard. It's certainly a work ethic that has trickled down to the next generation. Fresco by Scotto is owned and operated by "Mama" Marion Scotto; Rosanna, the coanchor of *Fox 5 News at 6*; Elaina, a former public relations executive, who has worked for prominent fashion designers such as Yves Saint Laurent; John, who was a nightclub owner in Los Angeles; and Anthony Jr., who developed the California franchise for Bobby Rubino's Restaurant on Fisherman's Wharf in San Francisco. Under their management, Fresco by Scotto has received outstanding reviews in *New York* magazine, *Gourmet* magazine, and the *New York Times*, as well as three stars in *Crain's New York Business*. The Scotto family is frequently featured on NBC's *Today*, where they demonstrate how to make an array of their mouthwatering dishes. On top of running a restaurant and pursuing their other career interests, the Scotto family is involved in the Jay Monahan Center for Gastrointestinal Health and the Food Allergy Initiative.

Marion acknowledged that as the mother of four young children—she had three children in four years; Elaina, the fourth, came five years later—juggling a household and coping with daily tasks was an art. "It wasn't always easy to make time for activities such as reading, but I tried very hard." She described their home as one filled with built-in playmates. "Of course I played with them as well," she recalled. Still, as a busy, social mother, it wasn't her only priority. "I had to take care of things, so I sometimes had to talk on the phone while they played." Community, Marion said, mainly stemmed from her group of friends who all had children the same age as hers.

As for her parenting philosophy, Marion described it as one that wasn't defined by nudging and prodding. "I had high expectations. However, that didn't mean I pushed them. I let them make their own choices." Explaining her parenting style as a medley—supportive, nurturing, and controlling to a point—Marion said it was most defined by her desire to guide her kids. "I always told my children I was their mother, not their friend, which meant that I gave them strategic direction." When it came to praise and encouragement, Marion did not use a one-size-fits-all approach. Instead, she directed each child differently, depending on his or her specific interests and talents. "Rosanna wanted to be an actress; Anthony Jr., a restaurant owner; John, a lawyer; and Elaina wanted to be in the fashion industry, so I encouraged and praised each one accordingly."

For Marion, that sometimes meant urging her children to pursue their interests through a different avenue than they had originally intended. "Rosanna, for example, wanted to be an actress. My husband and I both guided her into the TV industry because we felt that being an actress isn't a stable or easy career." As for the rest of the Scotto children, she and her husband did the same type of counseling. "John, for example, loved to talk and help people. He decided to be a lawyer and did well, but when we decided to open Fresco, he wanted to open his own restaurant."

As a large, Italian family, the home (and the dinner table) was the center of the Scotto household. "My husband and I were in a very stable relationship. . . . We had dinner every night at six and spent weekends together at our country home in Woodstock, New York." Asked what made them such a cohesive unit, Marion said it was simple: "We believed in having respect and love for one another." Additionally, she ran a tight ship. "I wasn't laid back. When I said no, it meant no." In line with the tight-ship approach, the Scotto children were kept on a strict schedule. "They had breakfast, lunch, dinner, and homework time; everything was very, very regimented." There wasn't any waffling in the Scotto household, either. "My husband and I presented a unified front, and if we disagreed, we discussed it in private."

Reflecting on how her four children have become as successful as they are today, Marion said it came down to just "encouraging, guiding, and loving them. . . . I supported them in whatever situation came about." Support, though, was not a one-way street. Marion described her relationship with her children as "a support system for each other." As for her image of herself as a parent, Marion said it's the same one that has propelled her family into the success they enjoy today. "I see myself as a mother who tried to be as good as I could possibly be." It's fitting, then, that Marion said the phrase most repeated to the children when they were growing up was "Nothing stops us," which is certainly proof that if you say it enough—and believe it—it will come true.

Elaine Skaist

Mother of PAM SKAIST-LEVY

"If they fall down, help them back up and tell them you still love them."

*E*laine Skaist—the mother of Juicy Couture cofounder Pam Skaist-Levy—said that when Pam was in junior high school she would wear pretty outrageous outfits. "I always said to my husband, 'She is just expressing herself'—and look what happened!" Years later, in 1994, Pam, with friend Gela Nash-Taylor, started Travis Jeans, Inc., a line of maternity jeans, but soon expanded to terry, velour, cashmere, and fleece tracksuits—a line that has revolutionized women's casual wear. The Juicy tracksuit is a favorite of celebrities such as Madonna, Gwyneth Paltrow, Jennifer Lopez, and Britney Spears. In 2003, Liz Claiborne, Inc. purchased Juicy Couture and expanded the emergent brand into menswear, children's clothes, bathing suits, shoes, handbags, jewelry, and fragrance. Today, Juicy Couture grosses over $300 million in annual revenues. Juicy Couture was also the inspiration for Juicy Couture Barbie dolls, which wear the signature tracksuit pieces and other Juicy accessories.

Reflecting on Pam's upbringing, Elaine said her priority was to impart good values to Pam. "We were not overindulgent with Pam," Elaine said. "I didn't spend that much, even though we were more affluent than when I was growing up." Because her daughter was a premature baby, Elaine had to give more attention to Pam. "The first year I felt so sorry for my older daughter because Pam took so much of my time." Even though Pam didn't talk until she was eighteen months and walk until she was almost two years old, Elaine said she wasn't anxious about Pam's development. "I knew she was a preemie and would do things on her own timetable." Still, Elaine encouraged Pam's intellectual growth. "We read a lot," Elaine said. "At naptime, at the library, at bedtime . . . we were always just reading to them."

Because the Skaists lived in Southern California, being outdoors was an important part of Pam's childhood. "We lived in a cul-de-sac, and Pam was always outside running or skating or bike riding or wheeling baby carriages. They also got to swim almost year-round." Elaine said that Pam had more structured activities as well. "She went to preschool at three, dancing at five, and joined the swim team at nine." Characterizing her parenting style as "moderate," Elaine said she was only strict about the big things. "I didn't tolerate hitting or lying. But Pam was really just such a good girl."

Elaine said they are still an affectionate family today. "My husband and I have been married for forty-six years. There was just always a lot of physical expression of love in our house." She explained that it was a dynamic cultivated by the time they all spent together. "We would go to the beach, or the park, or San Diego; we went to museums and shows on Broadway. But when the kids had different activities, we would stay home with them." Elaine attributed it to the strong relationship she had with her husband. "I think our strong family foundation was built on the incredible partnership I had with my husband. We were just always in cahoots."

Elaine immediately recognized a creative streak in Pam as she was growing up. "She was always interested in art and photography and writing poems." Honing in on Pam's strength—her creativity—was Elaine's approach. "Pam wasn't an academic. If she got moderate grades, we were happy." She also nurtured Pam's social skills. "I always noticed how cooperatively she worked with people. At one time, she was cheerleading, managing a store, and working at Fred Siegel. She just always worked so well with people." Elaine credits Pam's social aptitude for the successes of her relationship with her business partner, Gela. "They are as close as any sisters I have known."

Even though Elaine noted Pam's talents—namely, creativity and social skills—she didn't try to guide Pam in a specific direction. "We really let Pam decide what direction to go in. She had a few careers in mind. One was acting, but then she decided not to pursue that." When Pam decided to go after a career in fashion, it was her parents who backed the initial venture. "It wasn't Juicy, but another business at first. We were just encouraging of whatever she wanted to do." Elaine said that there wasn't a single defining moment for Pam, but rather a series of moments that all came together to help her get where she is today. "She just marched to a different drummer. Pam was just special and the trendsetter with everything."

For Elaine, helping Pam reach the top was about concentrating on her strong points. "I think you just have to encourage what a child is good at, and give them lots and lots of love, which is the most important thing." The other part, she explained, is being there when things don't go right. "If they fall down, you have to help children get back up and tell them you still love them." Describing her image of herself as a parent, Elaine said, "I am just a very happy person and very proud of my children. I love my life."

Judy Slater

Mother of KELLY SLATER

"If you suffocate children, they tend to keep secrets."

*J*udy Slater—the mother of Kelly Slater, the most successful professional surfer in the history of the sport—always told her son, " 'Color inside the lines. All you have to do is stay inside the lines and you'll be successful,' and I wasn't just talking about winning. If you conduct yourself correctly, you can't help but earn the respect not only of your peers, but everyone who looks to model their life after yours." Today, there are many people looking to emulate Kelly, and for good reason. He is an unprecedented eight-time Association of Surfing Professionals World Champion, active in numerous charities, and a proud dad.

In May 2005, at the Billabong Tahiti Pro contest, Kelly became the first person to score two "perfect ten" rides. Kelly has also dabbled in entertainment, appearing for one season on *Baywatch*. In 2003, he came out with his autobiography, *Pipe Dreams: A Surfer's Journey*. Kelly makes time for a number of charities, including Reefcheck, Quiksilver Foundation, Space Coast Early

Intervention Center, Surfrider, and Heal the Bay. He has one daughter, Taylor.

Kelly was the middle child, the sandwiched sibling position often thought to be neglected in favor of the youngest and the oldest—but Judy said that wasn't the case with her son. "I paid equal attention to all of my kids. They are the absolute finest gifts I will receive in my life." And while the attention was spread evenly, Judy said she tried very hard to strike that elusive balance between participating in her children's lives and not hovering. She realized early on that her cardinal rule of parenting was not to hover: "If you suffocate children, they tend to keep secrets." As a result, Judy said, "They could tell me anything. I never wanted to impose my personality on them. I wanted them to be their own people." Her parenting approach also was informed by always trying to put herself in their shoes. "I remembered being a kid. . . . That's why I saw my role as someone who was there to give them the tools to make good decisions, not to make decisions for them. I realized, too, that I didn't always know everything about their world, so they needed to learn things on their own."

Kelly's childhood, though, included some tumultuous times. He witnessed his parents' marriage dissolve and the sale of his childhood house while it was under threat of foreclosure. Judy said that although this was a trying time for her family, she kept her wits about her. "I knew that even if we had to live in a tent, everything would be fine." Judy recalled, however, that it was a challenge to keep the motherly façade of "everything is going to be okay." "I was really scared during that time, but I made my kids think we were fine. I quit my job as a firefighter, which I loved, and took a job as a bartender. I made about thirty-five dollars a day." Throughout the separation, Judy was adamant about keeping Kelly and his siblings in Cocoa Beach, Florida, where they had grown up. "It was extremely important to me that my children have roots, and I did whatever I had to do to keep them there." To make that happen, Judy sometimes worked three jobs. "But it was worth it because the kids were happy and loved living there, even though we moved probably five or six times while they were growing up."

Judy said she always felt sorry for children whose mothers bragged about how they were able to read at three. "It was always my belief that kids who are pushed too hard to excel, at some point, start to resent it." Instead, her approach was, "there's the toilet, when you're ready, use it." Although this was counter to how Judy observed other mothers raising their children, she saw the merits in letting Kelly develop at his own pace. "Let me put it this way, Kelly didn't graduate from high school with a diaper on." As Judy described it, the Slater household was not about being coddled. "My kids knew that when it was bedtime, don't cry unless an alligator is dragging you out your window, and if you're hungry, you'll eat more tomorrow." Emblematic of how she set rules and boundaries without being overly controlling, Judy said she wasn't strict about TV, and as a result, Kelly didn't watch that much. "He was always too busy surfing." Judy added that with all the social and athletic activity, watching TV was really a secondary activity. "Kelly always had so many friends over." Reflecting back on how her household was a haven for children, Judy recalled how she used to join in on the fun. "They always used to ask me to come out and skateboard, and one time I actually did it. Then it occurred to me that I shouldn't be out there because I was afraid my supercompetitiveness would click in, so I just did it once!"

Above all, however, Judy said her overarching parenting goal was just to have her children be good people. "I wanted them to be the kind of people others wanted to be around. I could take my kids anywhere and not worry about them misbehaving." But Kelly and his siblings certainly weren't born that way. "I was a disciplinarian. My kids knew my limits." Asked how she was able to impose limits but still give her children space to be kids, Judy said, "I gave them lots of room to develop. I also had what I like to refer to as my 'hairy mother's eye.' They knew when enough was enough." Juggling three jobs and a household full of kids, Judy said she didn't have time to be involved in everything they did. "I was involved in everything they did *from a distance.* I had faith in my kids. I didn't need to be there all the time." Judy also didn't have time be there *all* the time. "I was very social myself. I was president of the Junior Woman's Club, and then I was asked to run for mayor." Declining the opportunity, Judy explained, "I wasn't interested in taking any more time away from the kids. . . . My happiest moments were spent with my kids."

Judy gave Kelly tons of encouragement and advice, both from the front line and the sidelines. Equipped with enough parenting slogans for a book of her own, Judy said her favorites were: "Marketing yourself begins when you walk out the door in the morning. Sports does not build character, it reveals it. You can never accomplish anything great in the world without passion. Vision is the art of seeing the invisible."

Dispensing her advice for other mothers about how to tap into and guide their child to success, Judy recalled a very gifted child who had a lot of promise. "His mother once called me and asked me how I raised Kelly. What did I do for him? How did I teach him to be so amazing? My take is that when a parent interferes too much, it hinders the child's development. As mothers, our job is to nurture, help them when they need it, teach them to make good decisions, and take care of their needs."

Leah Adler

Mother of STEVEN SPIELBERG

"Never lose your inner child."

When Leah Adler—the mother of the Steven Spielberg, one of the most prominent filmmakers in Hollywood—was asked whether she knew her son was going to be successful she said, "I never really thought about it like that. I thought maybe he would get a job in a supermarket as a carryout boy." While most fifteen-year-olds were actually working as carryout boys, Steven had completed his first movie, *Escape to Nowhere*, and by the time he was sixteen his production of *Firelight* was shown at a local movie theater. Years later, his production of *Amblin'* led to his becoming the youngest director ever to be signed to a long-term deal with a major Hollywood studio.

In the 1970s, Steven made his commercial film debut with *The Sugarland Express* and later became an international superstar with *Jaws* and *Close Encounters of the Third Kind*. Steven is responsible for some of the biggest blockbusters in movie history, including *E.T.*, *Raiders of the Lost Ark*, *Jurassic Park*, and *Schindler's List*, for which he won Academy Awards for Best Director and Best Picture.

He went on to make *Amistad*, *Saving Private Ryan*, the World War II miniseries *Band of Brothers*, *Artificial Intelligence*, *Minority Report*, *Catch Me If You Can*, and *Munich*, which received five Academy Award nominations and was Spielberg's sixth Best Director nomination. Steven is also the recipient of the Lifetime Achievement Award from the American Film Institute and the Irving G. Thalberg Award from the Academy of Motion Picture Arts and Sciences. He has dedicated himself and his resources to many philanthropic causes, including the Righteous Persons Foundation, which was established with the profits from *Schindler's List*, and the USC Shoah Foundation Institute for Visual History and Education, which has recorded over fifty thousand Holocaust survivors' testimonies. Steven is married to actress Kate Capshaw and is the father of seven children.

When Leah described her own parents and upbringing, the role models for a son who had the creative wherewithal to make his first movie at thirteen became clear. "Although it really could have been a dismal childhood, it was so full of color. My father was Russian and very into the arts and loved music. . . . He would never walk into a room; he would leap into a room like a Baryshnikov. We were poor and happy." Joy, as Leah described it, permeated her upbringing, including religion. "Shabbat," she said, "was the most glorious day in our house." Passing on the tradition, religion also played a significant role in her household. "We always lit candles and had Shabbat dinner. Although we weren't very religious, the kids were raised in a very traditional home."

Leah said that it was her mother, Steven's grandmother, who originally saw something in her grandson. "My mother, who was a highly intelligent woman, would say to me, 'Keep your eye on him. He's amazing.'" For a free spirit like Leah, however, it wasn't about pinpointing some abstract quality and honing in on it. Reflecting today, she said, "I don't think like that. If I saw it, I wouldn't have recognized it."

As a child who was always ahead of the curve, Steven was speaking "articulately" at a year. When most kids his age were playing with trucks or sports, Leah said Steven's childhood was more about making films in the backyard. "He came up with such weird things. I loved his crazy ideas." While other mothers were driving their children to Little League, Leah was involved in a different way. "I schlepped him wherever he wanted to go to shoot film. When he was twelve, he wanted to go to the desert and film, so I took him." As fitting for someone who would go on to become the most famous director of his generation, Steven was always the director in these situations. Leah said, "I didn't set the example. He directed me from the time he was very young." Asked about whether, and when, she read to him, Leah said there was no schedule, an approach that is certainly emblematic of her parenting style. "Whenever is the greatest time I know."

For Leah, being Steven's mother was about sharing his passion for movies. "I was always fired with this kind of creativity. I loved the birth of things." However, Leah was hardly a pushy, overbearing mother trying to make her son into a young film prodigy. More than anything, Leah said that her parenting style was as much defined by cultivating her own interests as it was about Steven. "I had my own agenda. I was busy with my own stuff. I would say to the kids, 'Don't kill each other,' when I would leave to do my own things." However, Leah was always there when it mattered. "I remember he used to get frightened, because he had such a vivid imagination. I would just hold him until he calmed down."

Leah described a zest and passion for everything she did in life—qualities her son certainly inherited. Comparing her enthusiasm to watching a storm ascend, Leah said, she loves watching things build. "I love excitement. When a storm is coming, you should see me." It was this image, she said, that encapsulated how she parented and how she approaches her life. "I live for the moment and never think about tomorrow or the day after."

Although an unusual energy certainly permeated Steven's childhood, Leah said there was also a sense of normalcy about the day-to-day routine. "We ate dinner together every night. It was important for us to do that because, as a family, we really ignite each other."

Leah said she has, and would, do anything to help Steven in his career, including ruining her brand-new kitchen cabinets. "We had just built this gorgeous house with ash cabinets and Steven was working on a film called *Firelight* . . . it was really quite a production. There was a scene where a bunch of cherries explode in a pressure cooker and I hurled the contents of all these cans of cherries on my ash cabinets and as they're slowing oozing down, he's filming. It was fabulous. I lived in the house for eight years, and I never got the cherry juice out of the cabinets. Every morning I'd get up with a sponge and clean it for eight years. I ruined my cabinets, but I was so thrilled with the shot he got."

Asked about her involvement in the more typical aspects of her son's life, Leah said, "I had the world's record as the one mom who did not join the PTA. I ruined the 100 percent membership rule." In lieu of spending time at PTA meetings, Leah took the kids on trips. "We traveled a lot. We did a lot of camping. I'm a camper, a real basic camper."

Reflecting on how she participated in Steven's enormous success, Leah said, "I always used to tell him that guilt is a wasted emotion . . . but we come by it honestly, because that's the Jewish part." Leah also credited her approach of treating her children as adults.

"I never lectured them. I talked to my children as friends, so the advice I gave came out as nonpushy, which is why I think they could take it to heart. I think most kids won't listen to things their parents say just because a parent said it. With Steven, and all my children, it was more of a friendship of give-and-take. I wanted them to think of me as their ally."

Particularly as her children got older and entered their teenage years, Leah conveyed a sense that she "got it." "I would always tell the kids if you go to a party and you're having a wonderful time, you should leave because they'll want more and then they'll call you again." It was this ability—to give advice that spoke to her children's needs at different points in their lives—that Leah said defined her parenting style. "I was the type of mother who would keep my kids out of school to go get chocolate sundaes because I wanted to hang out. . . . Above all, I never pushed them to do anything, including make their bed." But that didn't mean that everything always went smoothly. "We fought. We screamed, but we did it in a healthy way."

Leah also made a concerted effort to expose Steven to the complexity and humanity of the world—experiences that are certainly reflected in the breadth and depth of his films. "We were always adopting or picking up all kinds of people, whether it was the housekeeper or the child of alcoholic parents. . . . We were not class-distinct people. We never saw class. If we saw class, we actually gravitated toward the lower class, not the upper class. We just felt more comfortable there." Leah said that this is how Steven still lives his life. "Steve and Kate are frugal. They have middle-class values. They want their kids to grow up with values. And so, in order to grow up with values, particularly when you're a billionaire, you need to have restrictions. I think that Steven is, above all, someone who sees different people's points of view, whether it's middle class, whether it's someone struggling, or whether it's a lost kid."

As fitting for someone who interprets the world through such a creative lens, Leah said her experience of motherhood could be captured by a photograph she has of herself and her daughter Sue in the living room in their pajamas: "The picture was just so dramatic. I was just so swept up in the moment, which is how I am. I'm just very present."

Above all, Leah emphasized her commitment to just being who she was—a quality she certainly imparted to her children. "I just like being me. I like my role in life." For Leah, that has meant eternal youth to a certain degree. "I think some of my parenting success has come from the fact that I've never lost my inner child." Having a mother like Leah, who helped her son realize his dreams, has set in motion a much bigger chain of events. "Steven has always helped young filmmakers. I think he realized the importance of having someone believe in you." Distilling it all down to an apt metaphor, Leah said, "You have to let your kids lead. It's just like dancing."

Sara Jacobson

Mother of **GELA NASH-TAYLOR**

"I didn't want her to grow up to be dependent on anyone."

In a 2005 *BusinessWeek* article, Gela Nash-Taylor—the co-founder of the iconic sweatsuit brand Juicy Couture—was quoted saying, "We had our biggest honor this year. We're Barbies now!" Building a brand that was sold to Liz Claiborne in 2004 for a hefty sum of $53 million might have something to do with what Gela's mother, Sara Jacobson, calls Gela's "fiercely independent streak."

"She toilet trained herself," Sara said. Gela, along with her partner, Pam Skaist-Levy, launched Juicy Couture with a mere $200. They didn't draw salaries for two years. Today, Gela is seeing a huge return on her investment, with Juicy sales topping $300 million.

Gela lives in Los Angeles and the United Kingdom and is married to Duran Duran's John Taylor and has three children.

Sara explained that the source of Gela's dedication stems directly from her lineage. "I came from a blue-collar family. . . . My father was a truck driver in Israel, and I always saw that my father had a strong work ethic, so I think I have a very strong work ethic as a result." Sara, who was raised in Israel, described her own upbringing as nonreligious. "I raised Gela without any religion. We did the holidays, but nothing overtly religious."

As a stay-at-home mom, Sara said that not working outside the house was a decision she felt very strongly about: "I was always there for Gela and her two siblings." This was especially important because moving to new towns was a staple of Gela's childhood. "We moved a lot because of my husband's job." While being uprooted like this might have had an adverse effect on some, Sara said it was advantageous for Gela because "It made her more secure in adjusting to new places and dealing with new people."

By the time she was twenty-one, Sara had three children. According to Sara, as the middle of the three, Gela was extremely independent. "Gela was a very fast crawler. She was forever injuring herself, because she was so fearless. I thought she would never survive because of all the trips we had to take to the emergency room." Gela's independence was no accident. Throughout her life, Sara said this has been something she worked hard to cultivate. "I always told her two things: 'Don't depend on any man, and be able to put on the food, no matter where you are in the world.' I didn't want her to grow up to be dependent on anyone." To facilitate this independence, Sara also told Gela to find a profession she loved and get a college education.

Although it might seem like an archaic concept today, Sara said she let playtime happen organically. "I didn't have her in any scheduled lesson or playgroups. I really just let it happen." By the same token, she didn't encourage social activity, either. "I just let my kids be who they were." Encouragement, Sara said, was something she used sparingly. "When it was due, yes, I gave a lot of it. When it was not, I didn't give it. I had my opinions and let them be known."

As Sara tells it today, fashion was not the first, or obvious, career choice for Gela. "Gela wanted to be an actress," Sara recalled. "The fashion thing came much later." Reflecting back on the trajectory of Gela's enormous success, Sara said the seeds for Juicy Couture were planted during a very tumultuous time in Gela's life. "When Gela got divorced years back and had two small kids, she decided to start the business—in that moment of crisis." Marveling at her daughter's tenacity and strong will, Sara said, "*Incredible* cannot describe what Gela did at that very difficult moment in her life. She did it from scratch and I have nothing but admiration for her." Asked how she thought Gela accomplished so much, Sara said, "I think she is just very good in crises. Gela is good at pulling herself together and going in a positive way."

Sara attributed Gela's unstoppable success today as a result of something internal, not a consequence of maternal prodding. "I didn't push Gela. When she failed, she had to pick up the pieces herself. While I might have been upset if she didn't do well, I was never really involved in it."

For Sara, attributing Gela's success to one factor is difficult. Instead, she sees it as more of a collage. "I think it is a combination of a lot of things. I am a hard worker and I think she always saw that. I have a ranch out in Texas and I drive a tractor and am ranching cattle." Sara also saw Gela's work ethic stemming from her father as well. "He was a workaholic, just like Gela." Gela's father and mother not only provided her with a model of how to work hard, but with a parental stable unit as well. "We are married over fifty years," Sara said. Pointing to her half-century marriage as one source of what gave Gela grounding in the world, Sara said that although her husband traveled a lot, when he was home, he made it a priority to eat with the family.

Barbara Taylor

Mother of NIKKI TAYLOR

"I consider myself a lighthouse. My light is always on,
a guiding force."

*B*arbara Taylor—the mother of supermodel Nikki Taylor—said she always told her daughter, "If there is love and support, you will make it through this," advice that certainly rings true for a daughter who has weathered an equal number of hardships and successes. Nikki is one of the most famous models in history. She was a millionaire and president of her company, Nikki, Inc., at age sixteen. She has been featured on the covers of every major fashion magazine, including *Vogue, Seventeen, Elle,* and *Allure.* In 1992, Nikki became the first model spokesperson under eighteen to sign a major contract with CoverGirl. Nikki also had her own bestselling line of calendars. In 1992, Nikki founded the Begin Foundation for the Advancement of Women in Business, which helps women with business ideas who have limited resources. She lives in Tennessee with her two sons.

Barbara described her own upbringing as one that made her realize that one day you could have it all, and the next day it could all be gone. This, she said, colored the way she viewed parenting. "I had good times, and I had bad times. My father had a job and we lived really well, and then he lost his job and we didn't. It always made me realize that as long as there is love, you will make it."

Although Nikki hit all of the developmental milestones right on time, if not early, she just didn't like to read, Barbara recalled. "I really tried to read to her, but she just wouldn't sit still. She was more interested in going and playing. Books just weren't her thing." Instead, Barbara took her three girls for long bike rides. "We would ride up to a place and have lunch. . . . My girls also lived at the pool, and then their friends would come over and they'd all swim. Actually," Barbara said, "our house was the hub of the social network, and I liked it that way. In fact, I can hardly remember the girls ever going to their friends' houses."

Looking back, Barbara described a loose atmosphere at the Taylor household. "They really did as they wished. Of course they had things to do, but after they completed what they were supposed to do, they were free to go." In the same vein, Barbara said she didn't regiment playtime. "I never said to them, 'Let's do blocks, or let's do clay.' If it was there and they wanted to do it, they got involved." Barbara recalled as well that Nikki loved to play store as a little girl. "I think that's why she opened her own boutique." Describing a more simple time, Barbara reflected, "It was just amazing how we got through child rearing without all the contraptions people have today. Car seats alone need a technician to put them in! Back then, we didn't have any of that stuff."

For Barbara, expectations really just boiled down to wanting her daughter to be happy and healthy. "What more can one really expect from a child?" When Nikki got involved with modeling at age thirteen, Barbara likened it to seeing a child who is really good at a sport. This begged the question, "How could we not have helped her pursue it? We just supported her and put her with the best people that we could find." Aware of what a stroke of luck it was that Nikki got what Barbara termed a "one in a thousand" chance to model, she also recalled how the "water just parted when she walked into her first agency. It was really, really amazing. She had her first cover within three months."

Having a child in such an adult industry put Barbara, like any mother, a little on edge. "It was scary because she was very, very young. We always had adults with her until she was eighteen, and someone always traveled with her." Thinking back on it all today, Barbara mused, "She probably resented it! After a while, though, the people in the industry respected it. We just wanted to make sure that she didn't fall through the cracks." Seeing all the makeup artists, photographs, and set designers, Barbara said, "Made me really realize that it *does* take a village to raise a child!"

In fact, it was the reminder "Don't forget the little people" that Barbara credited for helping Nikki not only become famous but well liked. "I always, always told her not to forget the person who puts on your makeup, the people who set up your shoot; sometimes there were twenty to thirty people involved. . . . There are a lot of people behind the scenes. . . . Nikki learned to always say good-bye to these people and shake their hands. It helped her popularity." It's also something that Barbara models in her own life. "At the end of a movie, I like to watch the full credits, which sometimes roll on for ten minutes. I think it's important to acknowledge the people who are usually the silent entity."

When asked about family stability, Barbara said, "I married the best guy ever, and that's why we were probably always together as a family." Her forty-year marriage attests to that.

Revealing one of her "secrets" of parenting, Barbara said, "We just always kept the girls busy—it kept them out of trouble. When we lived in Miami there was a family skate every Saturday morning and we would go religiously. The girls loved to go, and Ken and I went to meet other parents there." When it came to church and Sunday school, Barbara didn't push it on Nikki. "I had a policy, though, that if we didn't go to church, that we would spend Sundays as a family. Today, Nikki has become really involved with the church and her boys really enjoy going."

While Nikki was wildly talented at so many things, Barbara said she was not an academic. "She worked at her own pace and her teachers were aware that she was a little slower than the rest of the kids. Nikki had a retention problem that held her back. If she was average, I was thrilled. I was just so happy that she had this talent and was able to make a nice living from it." Barbara recalled that it was the advice from one of Nikki's teachers that helped put this all in perspective for her. "The teacher told me, 'The goal is to get children to a place where they can live on their own. It doesn't always work out that they are going to be doctors or lawyers.' He made me feel a lot better about not sending her to college."

Still, Barbara was vigilant about not taking Nikki out of school for photo shoots. "One time the modeling agency called me, begging for Nikki, and at first I said no. Then I got a call from the editor of *Vogue*. I called her counselor at school who said to me, 'Can I go with her? I hate to admit it, but she is going to learn more that day than from any day at school.'" Her counselor was right. The photo shoot was in New York City, during the middle of a solidarity march for the troops serving in Desert Storm. "She marched with the navy that day. . . . I hope that memory sticks with her for life. I don't think a kid her age could imagine how many soldiers are over there fighting for our freedom, and she certainly got a firsthand taste of it."

Expressing her own enthusiasm about the incredible experiences and opportunities that were afforded to Nikki, Barbara said that was what defined her parenting style: sharing Nikki's excitement. "I think it's important to be a visual force in what they do. Even if you can't physically be there all the time, really show an interest." Barbara also stressed the value of setting limits for children who enter fields such as modeling. Instead of letting Nikki run wild with her fortune, Barbara set up a trust to protect her money. "We told her she couldn't touch it until she was a certain age."

Asked about how she has helped Nikki weather the traumas in her life—her sister Chrissy's tragic death, her almost fatal car accident, and the breakup of her marriage—Barbara doesn't skirt the fact that Nikki has been through a lot. "But if there is love there, you are going to go through," she said adamantly. "Even with Chrissy's death, her accident, and divorce, she is stronger for it today. Nikki values life in such a unique way." It's fitting, then, that Barbara used the metaphor of a lighthouse to describe herself. "I consider myself a lighthouse. My light is always on. I consider myself a guiding force. I am just a mom, though . . . but I am a good mom."

Nena Thurman

Mother of UMA THURMAN

"We learn from difficulties and obstacles; if you always spoil your children, you will weaken their character, instead of strengthening it."

Nena Thurman—the mother of actress and model Uma Thurman—said she wasn't your typical "baseball mom." So it's no surprise that Uma is not your typical actor. Uma has become one of Hollywood's most successful stars, commanding over $12.5 million a film. She has appeared in some of the biggest blockbusters in history, including *Get Shorty*, *Pulp Fiction*, and *Kill Bill*. In 2005, Uma became a spokeswoman for the French designer Louis Vuitton. Uma was recently named a knight of the Ordre des Arts in France—an award for outstanding achievement in the fields of art and literature. She has two children.

Following somewhat in her mother's footsteps—Nena was one of the top ten fashion models in the world when she was young—Uma has carved out her own space in the fashion world, and that's no accident. "Instead of being one of those parents who wants their child to be a lawyer because they were a lawyer, I was the opposite. I just thought a parent needs to provide the tools to help the child achieve what they want." Being raised in Sweden, a country known for its first-rate schools, impacted the emphasis Nena put on education for all of her four children. "Part of my upbringing in Sweden cultivated an attitude that a parent should give the best education to a child. The value of a good education was something that was very obvious to me."

Although Nena didn't have outside help when she was raising her children, she said her husband was always a willing partner. "He changed diapers and did other domestic things. . . . We raised the children together." Nena's husband, Robert Thurman, is a world-renowned scholar of religion, and the chairman of the Religious Studies Department at Columbia University. "Because of my husband's work, we often had Tibetan monks around. It was a different type of extended family." Although Uma had an atypical upbringing in one sense, Nena said that most of their home life was very "normal." "Even though it was a lively household, and a free upbringing, there was discipline. The kids had to go to bed at certain hours. It wasn't like a free-for-all. We ate together every night. . . . People had to wash dishes, rake leaves, and do other chores. They all had curfews." More than anything, Nena emphasized her deep commitment to motherhood, saying, "I didn't have a conflict of interest. My world was about being a mother for fifteen years. I was fortunate that I was able to do that because I had a career when I was so young. But I want to say that I admire women who have children and a career. I just had an unusual circumstance."

Nena—also a practicing Buddhist—said that her religious beliefs, coupled with her Swedish background, were the two main influences in how she approached parenting. "It's interesting how my Swedish upbringing went well with some of the Buddhist concepts. I believe that each person has his own destiny. When you find it, you just kind of know it." Nena said that from an early age Uma exhibited a very lucid idea of *her* destiny. "For example, she knew how to shop. When I took her into a shop, even when she was three or four, she would pull out the best clothes. She had this confidence about what she wanted to do . . . she was also very into theater."

As part of Nena's parenting approach of just being the enabler of a destiny, when Uma was fifteen and wanted to go to a special acting school in New York, Nena helped make that happen. "Although she was talented in theater, it wasn't me suggesting it. . . . We moved her to a school in New York City for children who are gifted and who do acting or other artistic activities."

In describing her unique parenting style, Nena emphasized how she always taught Uma to challenge and probe. "I always talked back to the TV. I didn't want Uma to think that everything she was hearing on TV was true. . . . I think it's important to bring children up so they investigate everything, and then they can make up their own mind. I think that is particular about how I parented." Quoting an ancient Buddhist book—the *Tao Tze Ching*—Nena encapsulates how she views her role as a parent. "It is an old book that says that parents are the innkeepers at the crossroads, and children are guests who spend a couple of days and then they take off again on their own journey. It is a metaphor that parents don't own their children. I always had that sense. That doesn't mean you don't have a close-knit relationship."

Although religion was front and center in her life, Nena said she and her husband didn't indoctrinate their children with their own religious beliefs; instead she gave Uma information to make her own decisions. "Today, they are not churchgoing Buddhists, and I'm not sure if being raised in a Buddhist household has anything to do with Uma's success." Nena said she used religion, and all subjects for that matter, as points of inquiry about the world. "We talked about everything. Our household was an intellectually stimulating atmosphere that was always open to questioning." Exposure to a wide variety of people and places was the foundation of Uma's upbringing. "We traveled abroad. . . . We went to Japan for six months. Uma went to school in India for six months."

With part of a parenting style with roots in Eastern philosophy and religion, Nena said she didn't have high expectations. "Of course I wanted her to be successful, but becoming successful is a very interesting thing. There are maybe ten thousand talented actresses out there, and only a few of them make it. So I realized how hard it is. There is only so much room at the top." Recognizing that "making it" involves more than talent, Nena believed it was Uma's talent coupled with her own good fortune that got her a break in the film industry.

When it came to encouraging Uma, Nena said she didn't really have to do that much. "Uma was determined and aware of what she was doing. She told me that she wanted to make her own decisions. I just told her to rely on herself, and that 'I love you with all my heart, and that I will always be there.' Whatever it was, Uma knew she could come to us." In light of all of this, it's no surprise that Nena said she didn't push her children. "Of course, though, if someone needed a tutor, someone would get a tutor. We did whatever we needed to do to get them over some hump."

Reflecting on Uma's success, Nena circled back to individual destiny. "I think, as a parent, you can have some influence on it, but you can't create a Mozart. Someone is born a Mozart." Despite all she has accomplished as a parent, Nena said that in hindsight, and with the valuable distance that yields perspective, she should have used more discipline. "I'll put it this way; if you always spoil your children, you will weaken their character, instead of strengthening it. We also don't learn by everything being easy. We learn from difficulties and obstacles."

Lynn Harless

Mother of JUSTIN TIMBERLAKE

"Different is good. No one ever stood out in a flock."

*L*ynn Harless, the mother of Justin Timberlake, Grammy and Emmy Award–winning entertainer and former member of 'N Sync, says that music is in their family's genes. "My father, Justin's grandfather, was the leader of the Memphis Fire Department Band, and as a child I grew up with their rehearsals in our house." Lynn, though, wasn't just a bystander. "I played every instrument in my high school band, and was awarded a music scholarship to college."

It's from this musical legacy that Justin Timberlake has become "Justin Timberlake." After creating a name for himself with 'N Sync, Justin went on to debut his solo album, *Justified*, and his sophomore album, *FutureSex/LoveSounds*. His success continued with his number one U.S. hit singles "SexyBack," "My Love," "What Goes Around . . . ," "Summer Love," and "LoveStoned," making Justin the male artist with the most consecutive number one hit singles from one album. Justin has sold more than fourteen million albums. In addition to making it to the top of the charts, Justin has become an entrepreneur with varied business ventures. In 2005, he launched the William Rast clothing line, with childhood friend Trace Ayala. Justin opened his record label, Tennman Records, in 2006. His film credits include *Shrek the Third* and *Alpha Dog* and *Love Guru* with Mike Meyers. Justin has produced multiple songs for a variety of artists ranging from Madonna, Duran Duran, 50 Cent, and Reba McEntire.

Lynn says that being raised in a middleclass neighborhood in Memphis, Tennessee, had a significant influence on her parenting style. "My father was a fireman and my mother sold real estate. . . . They struggled to give us all the things that we wanted. As a result, I had a deep sense of how far they had come." Lynn has always lived right next door to her parents so Justin was constantly surrounded by family. Today, Lynn still lives right next door to her parents.

Friends, however, were an equally important part of Justin's upbringing. In fact, Lynn said their friends were almost like family. "My best friend, whose son, Trace, is still Justin's best friend, helped me take care of Justin when he was little. I've been best friends with her since I was in high school." Today, Lynn calls all of her friends "our chosen family." "We are still best friends after all these years. Now we are into the third generation of that extended family!"

Even though Justin had his "chosen" family, he was officially raised as an only child. Lynn said she did her best to curtail the "only child pressure" to overachieve. "I always said to him to do his 'best,' but his 'best' might be very different from someone else's 'best.'" Lynn's other parenting mantra was: do the right thing. "Doing the right thing might not be the most popular thing, but I always told Justin to go with his gut and when your back is against the wall, you do the right thing." Developmentally, Justin was also way ahead of the curve. Lynn recalled of his early childhood years that, "He was speaking in full paragraphs when he was one!" Admitting that she might have coddled Justin just a bit, Lynn said she stood over him until he was four months old, prompting him to say "Mamma."

Even though Justin spoke at an early age, Lynn said that didn't translate into a love of reading. "Justin hated to read, so we ordered him a subscription to *Sports Illustrated Kids* and that got him to look at a printed word." She also found other creative ways to get Justin over his reading resistance. "My husband bought Justin some Wal-Mart stock, so he got in the habit of looking at the paper every day to see how his stock was doing." It worked! "Academically he always did really well," Lynn recalled, thinking of all those A's on his report card. "But it wasn't because he was pushed. Justin was inherently one of those kids who wanted to be the best at everything." And although it sounds like one of those legends parents tell their kids to encourage them to do their homework, Lynn swore that Justin always did his homework before he came home from school.

Reflecting on how Lynn cultivated Justin's independence and success, she said it was all about establishing trust. "When he was growing up, I told Justin, 'I trust you, until you prove to me that I can't.' So he felt responsible for himself—and I think he made wise, thoughtful decisions because of that." Lynn's parenting philosophy was the opposite of "be seen and not heard." As she put it, her goal was to make Justin feel that his opinion was valid. "We wanted him to know that he had a vote and that he was just as important a part of the family as everyone else."

Asked if there was an "Aha!" moment when she saw that Justin would one day go on to redefine popular music and sell millions of records, Lynn said it was when she heard her son and his four friends perform a song by New Kids on the Block at their elementary school talent show. "Justin was actually taking voice lessons, with my encouragement, at the time and he had an amazing voice and he sang 'I'll Be Loving You Forever.' That's when it clicked for me."

Reflecting further, Lynn recalled, "When we were at the Blue Grass Festival, when Justin was about two years old, he would play his little plastic guitar and banjo and anytime the band was playing he would stand there with them and hold his guitar upside down and backwards." Not only did Justin emulate the moves of the musicians on stage, Lynn remembered that he had an uncanny ability to sing at a young age. "Justin would always sing the harmony part to songs on the radio, which is something that his father always used to do, too. So I guess you pick up things from your parents. But everyone in both of our families was so musical that it didn't come as a surprise that he had the knack for it."

Considering Justin's wealth of talent, it's hardly a surprise to learn that Lynn gave her son a lot of praise and encouragement, but never in an overindulgent way. "It was just my style of raising a child to encourage him. I had a magnet on my refrigerator that said, 'If a child lives with criticism, they learn to criticize, but if a child lives with praise, they learn to accept themselves.'" Putting her parenting philosophies into practice meant family dinner together and staying involved with Justin's school and their church. "We ate dinner together every night. I was involved in the PTA and the church. In fact, his grandfather on his father's side was the pastor of our church."

Pinpointing the glue that held her family together, Lynn said it was definitely all about fostering good communication. "We'd talk about everything. My husband and I were really good friends before we got married, and that helped us form a solid model of communication for Justin." However, this wasn't just a talking household. As Lynn describes it today, they were always on the go. "We used to take Justin everywhere. There was a children's museum in Memphis that we used to go to a lot. And when we were home, we were always doing craft projects."

Lynn said her advice to mothers today is simple: don't be a stage mother. "No matter what it was, I always wanted Justin to have a choice. It wasn't about me pushing Justin." Asked about her role in helping her son get where he is today, Lynn said she guided him by instilling in her son the importance and value of commitment. "When Justin started voice lessons, we didn't have a lot of money and we were struggling to make ends meet. I told him that if he wanted to take the lessons he had to be committed." It was also his mother's wise words that "nobody ever stood out in the flock" that Lynn said shaped her rock-star son. "You know, everybody thought Einstein was a quack. I always told Justin that different is good." But it was never Lynn's aspiration to have Justin be the most famous or talented singer in the room. "What I expect of him, which I repeat over and over again, is that when somebody walks away from a situation with Justin, I want them to say, 'He is one of the nicest people I've ever met and I would love to work with him again.'"

Describing how she sees herself as a mother, Lynn said a recent Mother's Day note from Justin captures it better than her words ever could: "You are my teacher, my friend, and my confidante. I don't know anyone else who can say that about their mother. I love you so much . . . Love, Justin."

Marjorie Williams
Mother of MONTEL WILLIAMS

"Let your children know that you aren't perfect and you don't expect them to be perfect."

Marjorie Williams—the mother of talk-show host Montel Williams—said that when Montel was in high school he was already showing signs of becoming someone who would thrive in a career centered on helping people with life's challenges. "He was always the kid everyone came to talk to if they had a problem. If there was an argument in school, he would step in and stop it." Montel, though, took a somewhat circuitous route to the career of television talk-show host. After graduating from high school in 1974, he enlisted in the United States Marine Corps. Within six months, he was promoted twice, and in 1975 Montel became the first African-American marine selected to the Naval Academy Preparatory School. Montel left the Marines with numerous honors, including the Armed Forces Expeditionary Medal and two Humanitarian Service Medals.

In 1991, Montel began hosting his own show—*The Montel Williams Show*. He has since branched out into other areas of TV—producing a series called *Matt Waters* and playing a judge on the ABC soap opera *All My Children*. As well as successes, Montel has endured hardships. In 1999, he was diagnosed with multiple sclerosis, but that has hardly slowed him down. *The Montel Williams Show* was nominated for a Daytime Emmy Award in 2001 and 2002 as well as for the Outstanding Talk Show Host Award in 2002. Montel has four children.

Montel's mom, Marjorie, was one of four girls. Describing her upbringing, being raised by a single father in Baltimore, Maryland, Marjorie recalled, "What I remember most about growing up is that every Sunday you had to go to church." Remembering the community-oriented neighborhood she was raised in, Marjorie described it as a "family block. . . . Like they say, 'It takes a village to raise a child,' and everyone pitched in when I was growing up."

When Montel was born on July 3, 1956, he became the youngest of four children. As one of two working parents—Marjorie was a nurse's aid and his father, Herbert, was a firefighter—Marjorie said it was a challenge trying to balance work, life, and four kids. "All of the kids were active in school. I drove them to and from all of their activities." In fact, getting her children involved with school clubs was always a priority for Marjorie. "My only stipulation was that if you joined a club, you had to go visit before you signed up. Then, you had a responsibility to stay for a year in that club. I wanted my kids to understand that if you made a commitment, you had to stick with it." This was an approach that Marjorie said helped Montel become the first African-American president of his high school, Andover High School. Even as the high achiever that he was—president of his class and star student—Marjorie said she was very aware of not pushing too hard. "I found that sometimes if you push too hard, it has the opposite effect. All parents want their kids to do well in school, but sometimes they buckle under the pressure."

Reading, however, was an area she prodded and pushed at a little more. "I really encouraged reading books. They used to have book fairs at the local school, and I would go when it was almost over, so the books that were two or three dollars were now fifty cents. I would bring them home and the kids would read to me, I would read to them, or they would read to themselves." But it wasn't all books and no play. A believer in moderation, Marjorie allowed Montel and his siblings to watch television. "It wasn't the kind of stuff that is on TV today, and they didn't watch that much of it."

In the Williams household, every other Sunday was strictly designated as family time. "After church, we would go to the beach, because the kids loved to swim. We would spend the day at the beach, just playing with the kids, watching them swim." As someone who enjoyed social activity herself, Marjorie encouraged Montel and his siblings to invite their friends along on these family outings. "The only rule was that I made sure their parents knew where they were!" On the nonbeach weekends, Marjorie took Montel and his siblings to museums and plays. "Whether it was our church or another church, there was always something for me to expose them to." As Montel got older, Marjorie found another social outlet that she encouraged him to be a part of: "People to People." "Montel joined 'People to People' in the eleventh grade, a program where students from different countries came to stay at your house. Montel was even able to take a trip overseas to Prague as part of the exchange."

When it came to giving encouragement, Marjorie said she always told Montel that he could be anything he wanted; all he had to do was go for it. She did have two caveats, however: "You just need the education to get it. There is no limit to what you can do with an education. And not everyone gets it on the first try."

Like most working mothers, Marjorie had two shifts: one at work and one at home. Asked how she was able to balance it, she said, "Even though I worked, I tried to be there to help out, and my kids knew that." Reflecting back on just how she did manage to do it all, Marjorie explained, "I remember one year, Montel's school was having a Christmas program and he offered me, and only me, to iron these dozens of angel wings. I told him the next time I should share it with someone else! But he was so proud when he took those wings back to school the next day." Marjorie said that the balancing act was made easier by her boss, whom she described as "very understanding." "If one of my children was having a problem, I could leave my job. I was able to go to every parent-teacher meeting."

Crediting her fifty-seven-year marriage as the bedrock of their tight-knit family, Marjorie said that it's a marriage based on "respect" and "space." In addition, the Williamses' values were aligned. "Herbert and I both placed an enormous importance on family time. We ate dinner together every day, unless someone had something at school, and weekends we all ate together." While she described their parental duties as "equal," Marjorie said she was more in between "strict and laid back," whereas her husband was more on the "strict" end of the spectrum. "I allowed my kids to make mistakes. I know that everything doesn't go smoothly, but I held to my punishments. They were reasonable, though."

Montel's ability to connect and relate to people became the material he shaped his career out of, but it wasn't the career path he tried initially. "Just like Montel would talk to anyone with a problem, we took that same model with Montel. When he was about to graduate from high school with a full college scholarship, he said he wasn't ready to have such an unstructured life. He said, 'Mamma, I want to join the Marines.' So we signed the papers for him to do it."

In addition to open channels of communication and a genuine trust in Montel and his decisions, Marjorie said she believes she played a part in where Montel is today by just being there. "I was there when he needed me—Saturday, Sunday, any day of the week. I knew I couldn't be there all the time and that doesn't matter, but I was there to answer his questions and help him in difficult times." Asked about how Montel has overcome his battle with MS, Marjorie said, "Even though he has MS, he makes sure you know that MS doesn't have him." Boiling down the approach that has contributed to such a positive outlook, Marjorie said that she thinks it was about *how* she handled the difficult moments. "When I made a mistake, I let them know it. I always told them, 'we should have done this or that.' My advice is: Let your children know that you aren't perfect and you don't expect them to be perfect." Describing the image she has of herself as a mother, Marjorie said, "It wouldn't take me one second to give my life for one of them."

Arline Zucker

Mother of JEFF ZUCKER

"I didn't want my kids to live through me. I wanted them to love
what they do. But I think the one thing I always knew was that
I wanted kids who could stand on their own two feet."

*A*rline Zucker, the mother of Jeff Zucker, president and CEO
of NBC Universal, said that when Jeff was growing up she
never watched the *Today* show, because Jeff always wanted to
tune in to the locally syndicated *Skipper Chuck Show*. Ironically, Jeff
went on to become the youngest executive producer in the history
of *Today*. In fact, under Jeff's leadership, *Today* became the nation's
most-watched morning news program. Moving quickly from executive producer to entertainment president to CEO in 2005, Jeff has
put his mark on NBC with megahits including *Las Vegas, Law & Order,
Scrubs, Fear Factor,* and *The Apprentice*. This five-time Emmy Award
winner is also a husband with four children.

Although Jeff has reached amazing levels of success, Arline said she was always content with what they had—there was not a sense of wanting more or competing with the Joneses. "I don't think we ever thought that we didn't have something, because we really had everything we needed." Still, this hardly meant that Arline was complacent. "We would always tell Jeff to reach for the stars. He was capable of doing it, and we saw that."

Throughout his childhood, Arline modeled a strong work ethic for Jeff. She held a job almost straight through her pregnancy. "I taught school and I worked until February and Jeff was born in April." Arline said teaching was more than just "a job." "I really loved what I did." Arline parented by example, actively involving herself in the community. "I always did a lot of volunteer work, and I worked for the Equal Rights Amendment in the state of Florida." Reflecting on how all of this impacted Jeff, Arline said, "I think he recognized that we were hard workers. We don't show off a lot. We live very quietly. We just did what had to be done."

In addition to community involvement, Arline and her husband modeled a partnership in their marriage—a marriage that has spanned more than four decades. "I didn't have a baby nurse after my kids were born because my husband helped. I could say I never got up for one night of feeding. We discussed it and he said, 'If we're not getting a baby nurse, I'll take care of the nights.'" Their teamwork extended throughout Jeff's upbringing. "My husband would read to him one night, and then I would read to him the next. It was like whoever had the time."

Like most parents whose children don't reach milestones when they are "supposed" to, Arline was nervous that Jeff did things on his own timetable. "He did everything late, he got his first tooth late, and he talked much later. Jeff actually didn't talk until after I put him in prekindergarten, but when he started speaking he actually spoke in sentences." Still, Arline described a balanced approach in how she raised Jeff. "My husband and I were not fanatics about things."

Mother Nurture

Arline said she let Jeff develop at his own pace, but always encouraged his interests. For instance, seeing Jeff's affinity for putting together puzzles—a skill he would use throughout life as a CEO, making all the parts of the company create a whole—Arline said she couldn't buy him enough puzzles. "He would go through these three-hundred- and five-hundred-piece puzzles so fast."

Although Arline gave Jeff a lot of rope growing up, she recognized his talents and took steps to nurture them. "Jeff used to stand and wait in the morning for the postman, and he got so excited when he saw the postman and he wanted to interact with him. And I said, 'You know, he just really likes to interact with people. I think he would benefit by being in school.' So he was in school before he was two and a half."

Since she didn't have the hundreds of self-help books and television experts that parents have today, Arline said she parented with her intuition. "Back then, there weren't books that would help you, so I just recognized that something was going on with him and he needed more stimulation. . . . He loved books. He loved to color. He had great hand-eye coordination."

To help Jeff develop his strengths, Arline said they spoke to him and treated him like an adult, which encouraged him to push his own limits. "I said to him, 'You have to get out of that diaper,' and I don't think it took two days." When it came to socializing, Arline said that even as a child Jeff exuded maturity beyond his years, because he had always been treated like a grown-up. "He was very adult as a little boy . . . so it wasn't that we had to say, 'Oh, come on Jeff, say hello.' We didn't have to do that."

While Arline described most of Jeff's motivation and talent evolving organically, the one area she actively cultivated was his independence. "That's the one thing my husband and I were very, very conscious of. We were very independent people, and I think we just really made this very conscious decision to raise independent children." Even from the time Jeff was little he exhibited signs of self-sufficiency—the type of independence he would use later in his life to realize his extremely ambitious goals at NBC. "I remember once I was sick, I had the flu . . . and Jeff came upstairs with two pieces of bread and said, 'I have my lunch.' He could do things for himself. He was very independent."

When it came to tennis, an area where Arline saw that Jeff had real talent, she encouraged and enabled him to pursue the sport. "He was talented and we recognized that. . . . We traveled great distances to get him to who we thought was a good coach. I would say growing up, after the age of six or seven, every weekend was a tennis tournament." More than just encouraging Jeff at tennis and shuttling him back and forth, Arline said the whole family took it up. "We'd be at the tennis court, and they'd be playing with their friends, and we'd be playing with our friends."

Arline said Jeff was his own self-motivator at school; however, as a parent, Arline did not take this as license to just sit back. "We were involved in the school. We went to all the parent-teacher conferences and teacher activities. My husband would even take off from the office to try to get to a volleyball game, so Jeff saw that we were always involved with him."

Jeff's motivation and desire to achieve sometimes gave way to his temper. "When he couldn't succeed, he got very upset." Arline said that although it was difficult to calm him down and even though they were nurturing parents, "We wouldn't put up with ugly behavior." Arline employed this policy of firm niceness with Jeff whenever he got frustrated or misbehaved.

Religion played a minimal role in Jeff's life, but Arline always insisted her children go to Sunday school. Her philosophy was that if you are going to reject something, you should reject it out of knowledge, not ignorance. "It's like saying you don't like food, but you've never tasted it. . . . Our kids had a choice about how they were going to react to their religion. . . . I can see that Jeff is now doing the same thing with his kids that we kind of did with him."

Using this approach of giving her kids the exposure to decide whether to reject or embrace their Judaism actually helped turn them toward it. "It's so interesting that of both my kids, one was bat mitzvahed, one was bar mitzvahed, and both were confirmed because they wanted to be."

Arline said their close-knit family was a key element in Jeff's upbringing. "We would eat dinner together as a family. Even if my husband had to go back to the hospital, he would come home to eat and then go back out again. . . . We would also spend weekends together at tennis tournaments." Having such a strong family foundation, Arline said, was critical to facing the hard times. "I had breast cancer at age forty-five, and I went through hell. We faced it together, as a family." Years later, when Jeff was diagnosed with colon cancer, the same family unity ensued. "Jeff had already seen us go through this kind of crisis." Arline said Jeff has replicated the model of his parents' devoted partnership in his own marriage. "When Jeff was sick, his wife, Caryn—who he had only been married to for six months—was really wonderful. Those times frequently pull families apart and you know . . . it didn't do it, in either case."

Arline credited a careful balance of letting Jeff have his independence, but also seeking out and developing his talents, for taking Jeff to the top of his field. "I didn't want my kids to live through me. I wanted them to love what they do. But I think the one thing I always knew was that I wanted kids who could stand on their own two feet."

EPILOGUE

After interviewing fifty-two mothers of some of the most accomplished and talented people in the world, I fully expected to solve the parenting brainteaser of how do you raise a well-adjusted, kind, generous, and high-achieving child in a world where pop stars garner as much media attention as natural disasters. Over the past two years, I've eagerly anticipated that "aha" moment of "It's the type of the breakfast cereal" or "It's the Mozart she listened to while she was doing her homework." Alas, though, no such revelation hit.

Ironically, my nonrevelation sparked my revelation. While I was searching for a grandiose parenting theory, I was missing the point. It's not in the big picture. What I kept coming back to was this deceptively simple concept: the mothers were *there* . . . they were present, whether it was hitting a T-ball, driving their kids to singing lessons, or devoting one day a weekend to spending time together. Each mother, in her own way, was present in mind, body, and soul.

I was struck by how many of the mothers caught their children's enthusiasm for an activity. Arline Zucker, the mother of NBC CEO Jeff Zucker, told me that when Jeff became interested in tennis, it inspired a family tradition of playing doubles every weekend. To me, this was such a vivid reminder of something I think parents

(I'm certainly guilty of this) often gloss over. We spend so much trying to get our kids excited about what we want them to be interested in that we forget to meet them on their court, both literally and figuratively. This is actually something the Bible discusses and cautions us as parents: "[A parent's] job is to raise our children to leave us. The children's job is to find their own path in life."

This might not sound like an answer to an algorithm as complicated as parenting, but that's the point. Parenting has somehow become such an intricate fret fest over our children's diets, toys, and educational development that we've forgotten some of the basics. In that spirit, here are the "basics" I've been reminded of during the two years I spent writing *Mother Nurture*. Set traditions for your family, even if it's just all sitting down once a week to have dinner; always let your kids know you love them; see your child as he or she is; show up and be accountable; and, above all, *be present*. I also kept coming back to another rudimentary concept, expressed in a poem written by a former child, called "When You Thought I Wasn't Looking," that captures so much of the wisdom I gleaned from these amazing mothers. The former child reminds us that children are watching and doing as you do, not as you say. "When you thought I wasn't looking, I saw you make a meal and take it to a friend who was sick, and I learned that we all have to help and take care of each other."

Finally, I'll leave you on this note. I was heartened to find out, as I'm sure you were, that most of the moms I interviewed did just fine without preschool French, Vivaldi for infants, flashcards for toddlers, and gluten-free bread. And perhaps the biggest lesson of all of this: motherhood is not about being perfect; it's just about being there.

ACKNOWLEDGMENTS

For all the people who helped to make *Mother Nurture* a reality: Hannah Seligson, for capturing the true essence of *Mother Nurture* and hearing my voice so clearly. Jamie Krauss, for making sometimes what seemed impossible possible. Erin Rivelis, for being patient and thorough. Laurie Chittenden, for taking on this project with as much excitement as I have for it, thank you for taking the time to understand my message. Debbie Stier, for your enthusiasm, passion, and being my biggest cheerleader; you understood before we even spoke a word. Brianne Halverson; Tavia Kowalchuk; Michael Barrs; Will Hinton; Adam Rochkind; Keri Levitt; Alison Brod; Doug Grad; Jennifer Miller, for believing and opening the door; Nancy Spielberg for introducing me to my idol; Sara Pilot; Stefani Greenfield; Emily Koch; Lauren Muss; Alexander Chudnoff; Lori Shabtai, Charlotte Blechman, Dari Alexander; Robert Tucker; Afshcnieh Latifi; Heidi Green; Caryn Zucker; Stacy Boniello; Kary Mcoul; Sue Naegle; Susan Carson; Ashley Badger; Jennifer Brustarr; Jahmal Dokes, Sherletta Moore, Juliet Dickey, Meg Graham, Christine Sanchez, Terry Prince, Alicia Sydney Whitfield; Jennifer Pinto; Nadine Petry, Shari Scharfer-Rollins, Carol Archer, Kristin Stark, Marvin Levy; Kimberly Connors, Leshelle Sargent, for being so kind and patient; Jen Davisson; Laura Morton. To all the mothers who so generously opened their hearts and shared their wisdom. To my mother who always loved me and believed in me. Thank you.

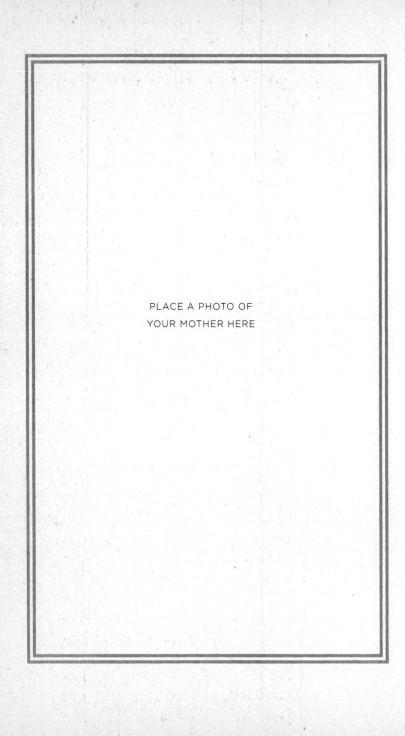

PLACE A PHOTO OF
YOUR MOTHER HERE

PLACE A PHOTO OF
YOU AND YOUR MOTHER HERE

Your Story

Mother Nurture is a celebration of motherhood.
If your mother deserves to be a part of this book, please
use the following pages to write a personalized essay
about her as a special acknowledgment for her love,
support, encouragement, and commitment in your life.
Enjoy reminiscing!

INCLUDE YOUR ESSAY HERE